Coastal Wetlands Restoration

This book examines a wide range of innovative approaches for coastal wetlands restoration and explains how we should use both academic research and practitioners' findings to influence learning, practice, policy and social change.

For conservationists, tidal flats and coastal wetlands are regarded as among the most important areas to conserve for the health of the entire oceanic environment. As the number of restoration projects all over the world increases, this book provides a unique assessment of coastal wetland restorations by examining existing community perceptions and by drawing on the knowledge and expertise of both academics and practitioners. Based on a four-year sociological study across three different cultural settings – England, Japan and Malaysia – the book investigates how citizens perceive the existing environment; how they discuss the risks and benefits of restoration projects; how perceptions change over time; and how governmental and non-governmental organisations work with the various community perceptions on the ground. By comparing and contrasting the results from these three countries, the book offers guidance for future conservation and restoration activities, with a specific view to working with local citizens to avoid conflict and obtain long-term investment.

This book will be of great interest to students and scholars of coastal restoration, wetland conservation and citizen science, as well as environmental sociology and environmental management more broadly. It will also be of use to practitioners and policymakers involved in environmental restoration projects.

Hiromi Yamashita is a professor at the Ritsumeikan Asia Pacific University (APU), Japan, visiting associate professor at Nagoya University Graduate School of Environmental Sciences, Japan, visiting associate professor, University of Cambridge, UK, and advisory board member for the Ramsar Regional Centre-East Asia.

Routledge Focus on Environment and Sustainability

Post-Pandemic Sustainable Tourism Management
The New Reality of Managing Ethical and Responsible Tourism
Tony O'Rourke and Marko Koščak

Consumption Corridors
Living a Good Life within Sustainable Limits
Doris Fuchs, Marlyne Sahakian, Tobias Gumbert, Antonietta Di Giulio, Michael Maniates, Sylvia Lorek and Antonia Graf

The Ecological Constitution
Reframing Environmental Law
Lynda Collins

Effective Forms of Environmental Diplomacy
Leila Nicolas and Elie Kallab

Coastal Wetlands Restoration
Public Perception and Community Development
Edited by Hiromi Yamashita

Sustainability in High-Excellence Italian Food and Wine
Laura Onofri

Learning to Live with Climate Change
From Anxiety to Transformation
Blanche Verlie

For more information about this series, please visit: www.routledge.com/Routledge-Focus-on-Environment-and-Sustainability/book-series/RFES

Coastal Wetlands Restoration

Public Perception and Community Development

Edited by Hiromi Yamashita

First published 2022
by Routledge
2 Park Square, Milton Park, Abingdon, Oxon OX14 4RN

and by Routledge
605 Third Avenue, New York, NY 10158

Routledge is an imprint of the Taylor & Francis Group, an informa business

British Library Cataloguing-in-Publication Data
A catalogue record for this book is available from the British Library

Library of Congress Cataloging-in-Publication Data
Names: Yamashita, Hiromi (Professor), editor.
Title: Coastal wetlands restoration : public perception and community development / edited by Hiromi Yamashita.
Description: Abingdon, Oxon ; New York, NY : Routledge, 2022. |
Series: Routledge focus on environment and sustainability |
Includes bibliographical references and index.
Identifiers: LCCN 2021013037 (print) | LCCN 2021013038 (ebook) |
Subjects: LCSH: Wetland restoration. | Wetland management. |
Coastal zonemanagement.
Classification: LCC QH76 C63 2022 (print) |
LCC QH76 (ebook) | DDC333.91/8153–dc23
LC record available at https://lccn.loc.gov/2021013037
LC ebook record available at https://lccn.loc.gov/2021013038

ISBN: 978-0-367-86308-1 (hbk)
ISBN: 978-0-367-76465-4 (pbk)
ISBN: 978-0-367-86309-8 (ebk)

DOI: 10.4324/9780367863098

Typeset in Times New Roman
by Newgen Publishing UK

Contents

List of figures vii
List of tables ix
About the contributors xi
Acknowledgements xv

1 Studying social perceptions of risks and benefits of coastal wetland restorations: Its importance and complexities 1
HIROMI YAMASHITA

2 Coastal wetland restoration in the world: Needs, challenges and benefits 17
ROBERT J. MCINNES

Case Study A information for Chapters 3 and 4: The Steart Coastal Managed Realignment Project, Steart Peninsula, Bridgwater, Somerset, UK 27
TIM MCGRATH, ROBERT J. MCINNES, AND HIROMI YAMASHITA

3 To enable communities to engage with the biggest European tidal flat and saltmarsh restoration project 33
TIM MCGRATH

4 People's perceptions towards the Steart Marshes Creation Project through stakeholder interviews and questionnaires 46
ROBERT J. MCINNES, MARK EVERARD AND HIROMI YAMASHITA

Case Study B information for Chapters 5 and 6: Kuala Gula Mangrove Rehabilitation Project, Kuala Gula, Perak District, Malaysia 61
BALU PERUMAL, HIROMI YAMASHITA, AND NAOYUKI MIKAMI

5 Local power through the Mangrove Rehabilitation Project in Kuala Gula, Malaysia 67
BALU PERUMAL, ALIFAH ILYANA BINTI MOHD HUSNI AND AMIRAH ADIBAH BINTI ADENAN

6 Community perceptions towards the risks and benefits of a mangrove restoration project: Learning from a case study in Malaysia 79
HIROMI YAMASHITA AND NAOYUKI MIKAMI

Case Study C information for Chapters 7, 8 and 9: Ago Bay Tidal Flat Restoration Projects, Shima City, Mie Prefecture, Japan 87
HIROMI YAMASHITA, NAOYUKI MIKAMI, HIDETO URANAKA, AND HIDEKI KOKUBU

7 The Ago Bay experience from a local government perspective 93
HIDETO URANAKA

8 Creating the first tidal flat restoration project in Japan in Ago Bay 103
HIDEKI KOKUBU

9 Tidal flat restoration projects in Shima City and citizens' perceptions 121
NAOYUKI MIKAMI AND HIROMI YAMASHITA

10 Opportunities for coastal wetland restoration and community development for the future 133
HIROMI YAMASHITA AND NAOYUKI MIKAMI

Appendix 1: Summary of the objective questionnaire sampling strategies in rural communities 147
Appendix 2: An example of the questionnaire contents (Steart Marshes) 153
Index 156

Figures

1.1 Ladder of participation for youth and citizens 3
1.2 Coastal wetland restoration method of re-introducing seawater onto land 5
A.1 Map of the Steart peninsula and the project area 29
A.2 Map of the Steart Marshes project 30
A.3 Aerial photographs before and after the restoration project on the Steart Peninsula 31
4.1 Personal/global and certain/uncertain risk benefit grid for stated benefits and risks in the interviews 49
4.2 Mental image of saltmarshes and mudflats at Steart Marshes 51
4.3 Perception of the functions of saltmarshes and mudflats at Steart Marshes 52
4.4 Degree of public agreement in overall project outcomes 56
B.1 Location of the Kuala Gula case study site 62
B.2 Map of the project site and constituency 63
5.1 Planting locations of various mangrove species at Teluk Rubiah 71
5.2 CSR groups' mangrove planting and educational activities 72
5.3 Shell crafts made by Friends of the Mangrove members 73
C.1 Shima City from the sky 88
C.2 Geographical features of Ago Bay 88
C.3 The four restoration sites in Shima City 89
7.1 Professional development training on the tidal flat restoration project at the Miyako Resort Okushima Aqua Forest Hotel 94
7.2 Changes in Shima City's population. 95
7.3 Shima City's coastal management approach, depicted through the properties of a pearl 96
8.1 An educational activity on one of the restored tidal flats 104

8.2 Distribution of the reclaimed areas around Ago Bay in 2010 105
8.3 Conceptual illustration of the trial design of tidal flat restoration 107
8.4 Outline of the same-scale trial site (Shaku-ura) 108
8.5 Seasonal changes in sediment quality and macro-benthos 109
8.6 The trial site (Ishibuchi) promoting tidal exchange by opening the floodgate 111
8.7 Seasonal changes of AVS, COD, mud contents and TOC 112
8.8 Seasonal change in species number and wet weight of macro-benthos 113
8.9 Complex governing structure around the coastal area in Japan 116
9.1 Removing sand dikes at the Wagu-ura tidal flat restoration site 122
D.1 Researchers in the field asking a person at the door 151

Tables

1.1 The typical logical flow of nature conservation and restoration 11
1.2 Differences between conservation and restoration 12
A.1 Background information on the Steart Marshes Management Project 28
4.1 Summary of the risks and benefits of the project expressed by the interviewees for the Steart case 48
4.2 Evidence of ecosystem service delivery associated with managed realignment projects 54
B.1 Kuala Gula Mangrove Rehabilitation Project details 63
B.2 Communities within Kuala Gula 65
6.1 Benefits identified by the interviewees in Kuala Gula 82
6.2 Changes of local perceptions towards the project from 2013 to 2017 83
6.3 Ecotourism approaches taken by Malay and Chinese communities 85
C.1 Details of the Shima City tidal flat restoration projects 90
8.1 The utilisation status of reclaimed areas and their characteristic appearance in 2005 and 2010 105
8.2 Annual characteristics of sediment quality (DL+0.5m) and macro-benthos in the trial sites before tidal exchange in Ago Bay 106
8.3 How different areas in the city are managed by separate governmental departments and mandates 117
9.1 Support rate of 'asari clams' as a success indicator across age groups 126
9.2 Awareness of and attitudes towards the restoration projects in Ago Bay 127
9.3 Importance of major policy targets recognised by the respondents 129

10.1 Citizens' judgement factors on restoration projects 136
10.2 Characteristics of citizens who tend to support coastal wetland restoration projects 138
10.3 Participatory success indicator development by citizens 140
10.4 Citizens' seven success indicators of coastal wetland restorations 141
D.1 Summary of the sampling and the case study sites 151

Contributors

Amirah Adibah Binti Adenan, Malaysia
Environmental Education Officer, Malaysian Nature Society (MNS)
Amirah has a BSc majored in ecology & biodiversity from the University of Malaya. At MNS, she is responsible for coordinating the national environmental education programme jointly conducted with the Ministry of Education, Malaysia. These include organising nature club activities in schools and developing modules for teachers' training. Her experience includes conducting education activities which are related to migratory birds and flyway conservation with local communities.

Mark Everard Ph.D., UK
Associate Professor of Ecosystem Services, University of West England, UK
Dr Mark Everard is Associate Professor of Ecosystem Services at the University of the West England Bristol. Mark's involvement and interests in the water environment go back many years, including formerly working for the Environment Agency and Defra in research and policy roles, in academia and in business, and with a strong interest in community co-management of natural resources in international development. Mark has been developing and working with ecosystem service concepts since the late 1980s. He has been a member of a number of intergovernmental (e.g. the Ramsar Convention Scientific and Technical Review Panel) as well as national and international expert groups. Mark has authored a diversity of scientific, technical and popular books, papers and presentations, and contributes to TV and radio.

Alifah Ilyana Binti Mohd Husni, Malaysia
Community Officer, Malaysian Nature Society
Alifah has a BSc in marine science from the Malaysia Terengganu. At MNS, she is responsible for developing community outreach programmes, and working with community organisations in wetlands conservation and restoration projects. Her experience includes the mangrove rehabilitation and conservation projects at Taman Alam Kuala Selangor and Kuala Gula, Perak.

Tim McGrath, UK
Senior Project Manager (Wetland Landscapes), ex-Steart Marsh Restoration Project Manager, Wildfowl & Wetlands Trust (WWT), UK
Tim joined the WWT, a non-governmental organisation for wetland conservation, in February 2009 with over 20 years' experience of working both with a number of country wildlife trust and the Rural Development Service. As an experienced naturalist with a long-time interest in ornithology and botany, Tim moved to WWT to manage habitat creation work across all of WWT's UK sites. In 2010, he became their full-time lead on the Environment Agency's Steart Coastal Management Project, one of the largest wetland habitat creation schemes in Europe. Following development and the construction of the breach in 2014, Tim turned his attention to coordinating the successful transition from construction site to a place for people and wildlife as WWT Steart Marshes became the first example of a landscape-scale working wetland.

Robert J. McInnes, UK
Director, RM Wetlands & Environment, UK; Associate Professor at the Institute for Land, Water and Society at Charles Sturt University, Australia
Rob McInnes is an independent chartered environmentalist and professional wetland scientist with over 25 years' experience in wetland-related environmental research, consultancy and conservation. Rob was previously Head of Wetland Conservation at the Wildfowl & Wetlands Trust (WWT) and has worked on over 400 wetland-related projects both within the UK and overseas. Rob regularly supports the work of intergovernmental agencies such as the Convention on Biological Diversity (CBD), The United Nations Educational, Scientific and Cultural Organization (UNESCO), UN-Habitat and the Ramsar Convention, as a Scientific and Technical Review Panel member. He is a former president of the European Chapter of the Society of Wetland Scientists and a recipient of the President's Service

and International Fellow Award for the significant contributions he has made in promoting wetlands conservation.

Naoyuki Mikami, Ph.D., Japan
Associate Professor, Hokkaido University, Japan
Naoyuki has visited all three case study sites with the editor and conducted the research activities for this book. His research interests involve environmental sociology, and science and technology studies, with particular focus on the sociological study of public participation in environmental and science/technology related issues. He has also coordinated a number of participatory exercises as a practitioner. His publications include a book on the participatory roundtable on the restoration of Sambanze Tidal Flat in Tokyo Bay.

Hideki Kokubu, Ph.D., Japan
Department of Environmental and Social Affairs, Water and Air Environment Division, Mie Prefectural Office, ex-Senior Researcher at the Mie Prefecture Fisheries Research Institute
Hideki majored in Applied Biosystems Engineering. He has extensive experience in tidal flat restoration projects, including the development of tidal flat restoration technologies and impact assessment tools for the restoration of coastal ecosystems. Also, as an experienced communicator, he has conducted restoration projects in collaboration with local citizens and government officials, and received the Civil Engineering Society Environmental Award (2002) and the Hitachi Environmental Foundation Special Environment Project Award (2014).

Balu Perumal, MSc, Malaysia
Head of Conservation, Malaysian Nature Society (The oldest and largest membership-based environmental non-governmental organisation in Malaysia, with 3,000 members)
A trained botanist by profession, Balu has a BSc from the University Kebangsaan Malaysia (1990) and a Master's from the University of Reading, United Kingdom (1993). Currently, he is responsible for running the wetlands, marine, forest and animal species programmes and is actively involved in conservation projects with local community groups, as well as the ratification of international conventions including Ramsar, CBD and the United Nations Framework Convention on Climate Change (UNFCCC) in Malaysia. He has more than 27 years of professional experience in natural resources management and environmental conservation in Malaysia, working

with three other environmental NGOs before joining MNS in 2012: World Wide Fund for Nature Malaysia, the Wetlands International Malaysia Programme and the Global Environment Centre.

Hideto Uranaka, Japan

Satoumi Instructor, Shima Nature School, Shima City; Ex-Deputy Manager, Department of Industrial Development and Promotion, Shima Municipal Office (previously the Head of Satoumi Promotion Office, Shima Municipal Office)

Hideto graduated from Mie University Faculty of Fisheries in March 1986. He studied at the Fisheries Department of Mie University and worked in seedling production as a technical officer at the Center for Cultural Fisheries of Mie Prefecture before he joined Ago-town office (now merged with Shima City). As the specialist for the development of fisheries for Mie Prefecture, he worked in the section for juvenile fish production, such as prawns and Japanese pufferfish. He began working for the project promoting aquaculture in Shima City in April 1989. He belonged to the section promoting satoumi between April 2011 and March 2019. He has made significant contributions to Shima City, which has received the Prime Minister's Award (2015).

Hiromi Yamashita Ph.D. (editor), Japan

Professor, Ritsumeikan Asia Pacific University, Japan; Visiting Associate Professor, Nagoya University Graduate School of Environmental Science, Japan; Visiting Associate Professor, University of Cambridge, UK

Hiromi's major is in environmental sociology. She is interested in public participation in decision making and how local knowledge can be utilised to form coastal development plans. Previously a member of the Ramsar Convention on Wetlands' Scientific and Technical Review Panel, currently she is an advisor for the Ramsar Regional Centre-East Asia. She has obtained Japanese government funding on three consecutive occasions to look at the relationships between local people and coastal wetland restoration projects on their shores.

Acknowledgements

As authors of this book, we are indebted to all the people who have generously given their time to our project activities, as well as encouraged us in many ways. We would like to thank everyone who participated in the interviews and questionnaires; your patience and insightful comments were invaluable.

UK

This survey received significant support from the residents and councillors of Steart, Stockland Bristol, Otterhampton and Combwich; the Sedgemoor District County Council; and the editorial teams and distributors of *Otter Tales* and *The Stockland Gate Post*. Throughout the research period, this project also received valuable help from the colleagues at the Steart Marshes Researchers group, the members of staff at the Environmental Agency Wessex and at the WWT Steart Marshes project, Alys Laver, Nicole Turnbull Wigley and volunteers, as well as at the Slimbridge headquarters, including the Working Wetland Landscapes Team, the Conservation Programmes, the Research Team and the Creative Services.

Malaysia

This work received important help from the following organisations and people: the Malaysian Nature Society, Global Environment Centre, Wetlands International Malaysia, Forest Research Institute Malaysia, the Department of Wildlife and National Parks (Centre for Kuala Gula Bird Sanctuary), Perak State Forestry Department (Site office at Kuala Gula), Sahabat Hutan Bakau Kuala Gula, Kerian District Office, Crawford Prentice, Anisah Binti Ahmad, Nabilah Binti Jamaludin, Mohamad Fadhirul Amin Bin Mohd Nor, Rashid Bin Ahmad, Puji

Astuti Binti Ismaun, Zakaria Bin Muhamed, Wahab Bin Arof, Tan Eng Chong, Siew Cheng Teoh, Ramesh A/L Sabapathy Munisamy, Lum Yat Kwai, Chńg Zhe Lín, Khoo Weng Kee, Tan Lip Thai, Tan Ming Xian, Tan Jie Sin, Tan Wei Yang, Tan Zng Chong, Nagarajan Rengasamy, Denise Cheah, Hyrul Izwan Mohd Husin and Sonny Wong.

Japan

The survey in Shima has received help and support from the Satoumi Promotion Office at the Department of Agriculture, Forestry and Fishery, the Planning and Policy Department, and other related departments at the Shima City Municipal Office, the Shima Environmental Conservation Office of Chubu Regional Environmental Office, Chubu Regional Environmental Office (Nagoya), the Mie Prefectural Fishery Research Institute, Shima City Tourism Association, Miyako Resort Okushima Aqua Forest, Wagu Residents' Association, Tategami Residents' Association, Seiya Harajyo, Yoshito Hamano, Hiroko Iwaki, Kazuhiro Iwaki, Tatsuya Sato, Kazuya Fujita, Syun Amemiya, Kiyotaka Uchida, Masako Otsuka, Yukimitsu Nakanishi, Hirokatsu Yamada, Osamu Matsuda and Susumu Takayama.

We are also very much indebted to Gerry Blunt, Graeme Douglas, Ryoichi Terada, Hiroto Nagai, Thu Huong Pham, Nick Davidson, Max Finlayson, Takumi, Mitsuko, Takehisa and Christopher Williams.

Funding

This book is based on work supported by JSPS Kakenhi Grant-in-Aid for Scientific Research (B) (Grant Number 15H02873): 'Development of new environmental communication model based on citizens' perceptions towards tidal flat restoration projects'.

1 Studying social perceptions of risks and benefits of coastal wetland restorations

Its importance and complexities

Hiromi Yamashita

1.1 Why study social perceptions?

People generally embrace the idea of going back to 'the good old days', a time when they were young and energetic, or perhaps when they had many thriving friends. Some of us have a similar feeling of excitement and positivity about 'restoring' nature. The concept of restoring nature, especially knowing the variety of benefits for nature and communities, is embraced by many. However, not all citizens are positive towards restoration ideas, which has puzzled many in local and national government and environmental non-government organisations (NGOs). With their questions unanswered, they continue trying to 'educate' such citizens, unsurprisingly, without success.

The content of this book is based on a sociological study of how citizens in different parts of the world perceive and discuss the risks, benefits and sense of fairness in coastal wetland restoration projects on their shores, and how these perceptions change over time. We had three main questions in mind before starting the in-depth case studies in England, Japan and Malaysia:

- How do people rationalise the risks and benefits of environmental restoration projects?
- How do people perceive a particular ecosystem to be restored?
- What are the implications of the findings for future practice and research?

This book does not take sides when comparing people who are for or against proposed environmental restoration projects, nor in concluding who is right, environmentalists or citizens. It presents how citizens are

DOI: 10.4324/9780367863098-1

constructing their attitudes towards coastal restoration projects and the reasons behind them, including the short- and long-term risks and benefits. The purpose of this book is to explore how to combine both academic research and practitioners' findings to influence practice, policy, research and communication, to reflect all concerns and expectations towards any project.

Many conservationists conclude that ensuring citizens are involved in decision making and understanding their concerns are important when conducting environmental projects. But in what way? Can such collaboration be truly helpful or useful, and if so, for whom? We consider this in three different contexts: the restoration project; the community and its members; and future restoration projects and environmental decision making.

Restoration projects need long-term investment, appreciation and financial support, as well as goodwill from local residents. Citizen participation benefits projects in various ways and the push for greater participation is being driven by considerable optimism about its ability to improve the substantive and procedural quality of decisions. Valuing public involvement in decision making could restore a degree of trust in agencies and project contractors, resolving conflict with residents and/or among competing local interests. As the German sociologist Ortwin Renn and his colleagues (1995, p. 3) mention, "while issues of values, conflict, and trust have long been considered key concepts in the study of public participation, most evaluations have not explicitly operationalized them into evaluative criteria".

Renn et al. (1995) argue that a traditional 'top-down' consultative participation style is often counterproductive and unsatisfactory to participants. However, attempts to include citizen participation are not free from power issues. Pimbert and Preetly (1994) list various types of participation in coastal zone management, demonstrating different levels of participation according to the power 'given to' or shared with citizens. They included passive participation, participation in information giving, participation by consultation, participation for material incentives, functional participation, interactive participation and self-mobilisation/active participation. Citizen participation in decision making could provide, "not only results but satisfaction and investment from their engagement in decision making" (Katz and Miller, 1996, pp. 133–134).

Hart's (1992 after Arnstein, 1969) classic 'ladder of participation' for young people has some relevance to citizen participation. However, he warns that at the lower levels, participation or even sharing knowledge

	***Ladder of participation* for youth**		***Ladder of participation for citizens***
Degrees of participation	8. Youth-initiated, shared decisions with adults		8. Citizen-initiated, shared decisions with authorities
	7. Youth-initiated and directed		7. Citizen-initiated and directed
	6. Adult-initiated, shared decisions with youth		6. Authorities-initiated, shared decisions with Citizens
	5. Consulted and informed		5. Consulted and informed
	4. Assigned but informed		4. Assigned but informed
Non-participation	3. Tokenism		3. Tokenism
	2. Decoration		2. Decoration
	1. Manipulation		1. Manipulation

Figure 1.1 Ladder of participation for youth and citizens (after Hart, 1992 and Arnstein, 1969).

with project workers is not really achieved. When we use the term 'participation', we need to be clear what that means.

Understanding citizens' perceptions of the risks and benefits towards a project helps a society to become reflective and ready for change in the future. In the current literature, participation may only refer to level five of Hart's levels of participation at the most (consulted and informed). For a community project, eight would be the ideal level of participation (citizen-initiated, shared decisions with authorities).

Encouraging citizens to be a part of or, even better, to be a leader of decision making creates an active environment where local people invest their time and thinking about their future environment more frequently and more deeply. However, often how other people or authorities support local people to climb up the ladder towards interdependence and empowerment is not discussed much in the literature. Understanding local people's perceptions of project ideas, government officials and their environment is one of the important factors in helping authorities to recognise their misconceptions about locals, which often hinders local people to climb up the participation ladder. Therefore, in this book, as well as looking at social perceptions of wetland restoration projects, we look at how authorities or organisations can encourage local participation and empowerment.

1.2 The coastal wetland restoration methods discussed in this book

A coastal wetland is a shallow, often muddy, part of the seashore, which is covered and uncovered by the rise and fall of the tide. It supports not only an immense variety of wildlife but also has an economic value, including providing a source of food, water purification, erosion control and mitigating damage from tsunamis. Among conservationists, tidal flats are regarded as one of the most important areas to conserve for the health of wider coastal and oceanic environments. International convention documents, such as those produced by the Ramsar Convention Secretariat (2018a) emphasise this. Coastal wetlands might not look particularly attractive, but due to their important functions, they are also known as the 'rainforest of the water', 'womb of the sea' and 'kidney of the earth'. Yet, their importance has not been recognised widely by the public and decision makers, and it is said that 63% or more of coastal wetlands have been lost to development and land use changes all over the world (Davidson, 2014; Ramsar Convention Secretariat, 2018b).

In recent years, however, various coastal wetland restoration projects have been conducted in the world to prepare for sea-level rise or to revitalise fish stocks (e.g. Environment Agency, 2021). Mitsch (2010), a wetland scientist, notes that ecological restoration is becoming common practice in improving the ecological quality of many degraded ecosystems. There are different types of restoration activity, including both hard and soft engineering. In this book, restoration is defined as "the process of assisting the recovery of an ecosystem that has been degraded, damaged, or destroyed", as defined by the Society of Ecological Restoration (SER, 2004, p. 3).

Across the world, the number of coastal realignment projects (restoring the original coastal line and creating coastal wetlands) has increased, utilising green infrastructures such as wetlands' water purification mechanism. These projects simultaneously provide protection against natural disasters, revitalise fishing grounds and prepare for global warming. For example, in the UK, 55 projects have already been completed, alongside about 100 projects in Europe (Esteves, 2014).

The content of this book is based on a Japanese government-funded research project, which looks at citizens' risk and benefit perceptions towards coastal wetland restoration. The three case studies share the same cost-effective, yet potentially controversial, restoration techniques of introducing seawater onto land previously used for farming or housing. The detailed background of each case study site will be discussed in later chapters.

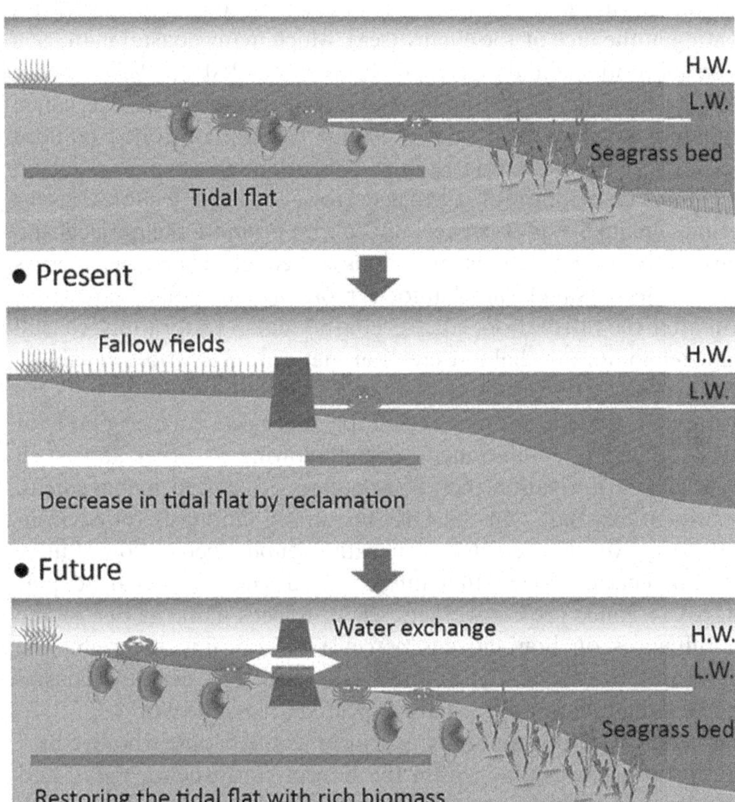

Figure 1.2 Coastal wetland restoration method of re-introducing seawater onto land (Mie Prefectural Fisheries Research Institute, 2012). (There is a sea wall blocking tidal flat to create fallow field. The figure showing creating a whole on the sea wall to crate water exchange between ex-fallow field and outer ocean to restore the tidal flat with rich biomass. H.W. means high water, L.W. means low water.)

1.3 Terms used for coastal wetland restorations

The process of 'setting back' the shoreline has been referred to by different names over time and by different projects. Currently, in England many of these projects are called 'managed realignments', whereby the coastal line is set back and the existing outer sea wall is breached. The restoration of tidal wetlands in the UK was initially referred to as 'setting back' before the rapid change to 'managed retreat'. However, it is now seen as unhelpful since, "it suggests a negativity in coastal management, 'retreating in the face of the enemy (sea)' which many coastal managers and coastal residents find unacceptable" (French, 2001, p. 271).

Such 're-flooding' to restore land to how it was might also be called de-embankment; regulated tidal exchange (RTE); controlled reduced tide (CRT); or de-poldering (in the Netherlands) when focused on the technical description of a project. However, these technical terms sometimes create distance between those who promote the projects and citizens, with few positive connotations for either. Therefore, various projects are now using terms that focus more on what citizens are going to gain after the restoration, such as coastal marsh restoration, coastal wetland rehabilitation, habitat creation, natural restoration, rewilding or tidal hydrology restoration.

Conversely, these terms may then imply a project's focus is purely or mainly biodiversity enhancement, overshadowing its other aims such as sea-level rise mitigation, flood prevention or erosion management. Esteves mentions that, "In the UK, the strong emphasis on environmental objectives has created a negative public perception. Public reaction reflects the views that interests and safety of local people" (2014, p. 22). Since project workers see a project's name as one of the main influences on how citizens perceive it, choosing the right one is important. Consequently, a variety of names to describe coastal managed realignment projects have appeared across the world.

In this book, local community is defined as the people who live by a restoration project, usually within the project constituency areas, and the people who utilise the restoration project related area for living such as fishery or farming. They are the people who share the same geographical location in their day-to-day lives, although they might not belong to the same organisations or share common values or perceptions of their wetlands. For wetland landscapes, 'local community' is a contested term, since users – both people and living creatures – may only visit these spaces periodically according to variations in the hydrologic regime or visiting species such as overwintering birds. Indeed, in terms of the ecology, community means "a group of interdependent plants and animals inhabiting the same region and interacting with each other through food and other relationships" (Collins Cobuild). However, in this book, we only look at 'local community' from human points of view, although, of course, the way all entities use wetlands changes periodically. In this study, we tried to understand community needs and resources, and how people perceive their environment including their perceptions of interconnection and interdependence, shared responsibility and possible common goals.

1.4 What does past research tell us about studying social perceptions?

Studying social perceptions of risks and benefits entails different disciplines, and this area of study is still relatively new. Coastal wetland restoration projects, such as coastal realignments or re-flooding farmland, also represent a new concept. However, it is likely to become an important environmental conservation activity in the future. Due to the need for long-term social support and investment in such schemes, as well as avoiding potential conflict, it is becoming increasingly important to take account of the various perceptions that exist in local communities.

To capture citizens' perceptions on these potentially controversial projects, the data collection methods were rigorously considered for this research project to ensure public opinion was gathered. Sociological studies on people's perceptions are rare in the field of coastal restoration; therefore, not only the results, but also the variety of rigorous research methods applied to collect data for this book in the different cultural settings could be of interest to readers and future researchers.

1.4.1 Current indicators of success for restoration projects

What defines success in a restoration project is not clear across various practices. One of the biggest natural restoration associations, the Society of Ecological Restoration (SER), has produced a primer to summarise the key elements inherent in all restoration projects (SER, 2004). It encourages direct comparison, and attribute and trajectory analysis of seven elements: (1) similar diversity and community structure in comparison with reference sites; (2) presence of indigenous species; (3) presence of functional groups necessary for long-term stability; (4) capacity of the physical environment to sustain reproducing populations; (5) normal functioning; (6) integration with the landscape; and (7) elimination of potential threats. However, research looking at projects across the world found that most evaluation criteria did not cover all the SER elements (SER, 2004).

To date, current indicators of the success of managed realignment projects often relate to the increase of biodiversity within the project area, such as this one from Japan. In terms of social perceptions, there are fewer studies., and Curado et al. point out that "Only a few restoration projects incorporate public perception in their monitoring" (2014, p. 668).

1.4.2 The general risk-benefit principle and its limitations

In deciding if a project is worthwhile, it is common to conduct a risk-benefit, or cost-benefit, analysis. Cost is often seen in monetary terms, so here we will use the term 'risk' since it includes non-monetary burdens on people. 'Risk' and 'benefit' are often discussed as a pair; however, while risk is perceived as probability × severity, benefit is often understood as something that will definitely happen, even though it should realistically be probability × gain. In addition, benefits are felt not only economically, but also psychologically, physically, socially and educationally, which are difficult to calculate in monetary terms.

There are various aspects of a common risk-benefit analysis that do not necessarily fit with restoration projects. Usually, the analysis requires a quantitative evaluation, most commonly in economic terms. Risk is often discussed in terms of human lives and injury while benefits can be calculated in economic terms, such as how much higher a yield is obtained if a particular pesticide is used. In deciding whether to take a risk, an individual or group (e.g. local government on behalf of local citizens) decides what is the cheapest option for maximum gain.

In managing societal risks, where risk and benefit principles cannot be applied to individuals, what kinds of compensation can be applied? This depends on how one can reconcile the efficiency obtained by applying the benefit principle with the fairness of risk benefit distribution (Oka, 1996). When individual property is lost or damaged, one can claim compensation; however, an individual might not be able to do so if common (shared) property is damaged when a risk becomes reality, even if they have lost personal property and income.

When the Belmont report talks about assessing risks/benefits in clinical research, it highlights the importance of respecting human rights and informed consent. This is firmly under the individual risk/benefit umbrella. Meanwhile, Gofman (1981) argues that having no choice about facing a certain risk without being consulted is a violation of human rights.

Terada (2016) argues that risk is often discussed together with benefit, and this might lead to the assumption that one must accept risks to obtain benefits (socially or individually). Therefore, people who actively participate in activities are taking risks for their chosen or understood benefits. However, if people do not accept the risk or are not reconciled with the reasoning behind an activity, they have risks imposed on them and the risks simply become 'dangers' (Luman, 1993).

The issue of risk and benefit arguments was an important element in examining the case study sites, since all the construction or development projects used the discourse of costs and benefits in taking certain risks with people and/or environments.

1.4.3 Past research on social perceptions of coastal wetland restoration projects

The number of restoration projects is increasing across the world, and the importance of understanding public opinion has been keenly discussed at many international conferences over the decades. This section looks at what kinds of discourses have been identified regarding perceptions of coastal wetland restoration projects (especially tidal flat restorations) in different parts of the world; the conclusions that have been drawn so far; and the contributions environmental sociological approaches could make in future studies.

To identify existing literature in this field, I searched articles in the following databases: Web of Science, EBSCO, SöderScholar, CiNii (Japanese academic article database) and the National Diet Library of Japan. The search key words included tidal flat, restoration, coastal realignment, social perception, risk and benefit (Yamashita, 2015). My aim was to look for peer-reviewed journal articles, as this system goes some way to ensure the research activities being reviewed are conducted to a certain standard. A total of 110 journal articles with links to social perception of tidal flat restorations, directly or indirectly, were found. Among these, only nine articles were directly concerned with social perception studies on tidal flat restoration projects; I have looked at these articles closely for this review.

The aims of restoration projects vary; for example, climate change mitigation, creation of areas for birds to breed and increasing biodiversity. However, all the reviewed studies mentioned the importance of researchers and project contractors looking into social perceptions of tidal flat restoration projects for future restoration work. All but one study employed questionnaire methods to understand citizens' perceptions. One study employed questionnaires together with a five-minute interview with participants (Curado et al., 2014) and one used in-depth interview methods with 15 respondents (Roca and Villares, 2012). Curado et al. (2014) note that, "only a few restoration projects incorporate public perception in their monitoring" (p. 668). England et al. (2008) agree that once a restoration project has been carried out, good monitoring is essential in improving the restoration methodology for future applications; however, monitoring of public perception has seldom been conducted.

Most of the studies note that citizens recognise the benefits of coastal marshes and tidal flats. However, the main discourse was based on a 'deficit model' regarding citizens. When looking at the study results closely, although they clearly list what kinds of opinions have been expressed by citizens, they lack investigation into aspects of environmental justice and risk communication. Citizens are sometimes branded as self-interested, hoping to receive short-term and tangible benefits without caring for tidal flat environments or future generations.

One of the strong commonalities across these perception studies' conclusions is citizens' lack of knowledge of the importance of tidal flat environments. Curado et al. (2014) mention that, "citizens recognized the benefits of coastal marshes, a perception which increased with increasing educational level" (p. 674). Goeldner-Gianella (2007) says, using the very direct term "the publics' scant knowledge", that knowledge of the environment and physical context must be improved if citizens are to better understand and accept any future de-polderisation projects (p. 1228).

Myatt et al. (2002, 2003a, 2003b, 2003c) agree that there is lack of public understanding on tidal flat environments and projects, and suggest education and communication are key revision areas for project implementers. They suggest that "regular newsletters or mail-drops (with diagrams) would be welcomed, thus reaching and informing wider audiences and those who are more reliant on this type of media as their only source of information" (Myatt et al., 2003a, p. 285). Esteves and Thomas (2014) recommend improving education efforts to reduce negativity associated with a 'give in to the sea' perception.

Unfortunately, all the above research findings encourage one-way communication: from the expert to the unknowing. It is a 'deficit model' that claims citizens would understand the importance of restorations if only they understood the information or knowledge 'correctly'. Roca and Villares (2012) claim, "more educational intervention and the provision of opportunities for participation are necessary to overcome the general lack of trust in institutions and fears regarding innovative coastal intervention methods" (p. 46). Myatt et al. note that, "In general, respondents agreed that the consultation process was a good opportunity for residents to express their interest and allay their fears to the 'expert'" (2003b, p. 580). However, they do not strongly emphasise the importance of institutions or implementers obtaining knowledge from citizens who are 'experts' in their environment and their perceptions of risks and benefits of a particular project.

As well as the issues of public perception, Goeldner-Gianella (2007) concludes that the constraints and obstacles associated with de-polderisation include insufficient financial compensation for landowners; overly strict environmental legislation; the loss of valuable land; and a lack of public support coupled with an absence of public consultation. Social perception is therefore only "one of the conditions for the acceptance and success of any de-polderisation process" (p. 1220). Myatt et al. (2003a, 2003b, 2003c) note the trust issue between citizens and a government agency could act as a barrier in promoting restoration projects.

However, the existing studies still lack investigation into why citizens express specific perceptions and opposition. The fact that most of the studies (seven out of nine) solely employed questionnaire methods might have also contributed to why these findings did not explore how and why citizens formed their various opinions.

1.5 The difference between 'restoration' and 'conservation' projects

There is a tendency for project workers and citizens to conflate the terms restoration and conservation. However, in the literature restoration does not necessarily equate with conservation, since in many ways they are different. Conservation mainly seeks to preserve current conditions, while restoration projects often have aims to achieve. For example, a coastal realignment's focus is not always reinstating a former environment, but rather developing an optimal solution for a clearly defined problem, such as coastal flooding, erosion or aquatic ecology improvement. The project logic of each activity is typically developed as below.

Table 1.1 The typical logical flow of nature conservation and restoration

Conservation	• Awareness of a particular nature → embracing it and understanding its value → (with or without) scarcity → conservation and actions of wise/sustainable use
Restoration	• Scarcity or complete loss of a particular nature → results in in-situ or ex-situ social issues → understanding of value of nature and what has been lost + additional justifications or problems to be solved (e.g. safety or economic reasons) = restoration projects happen → partially solving existing problems + creating nature to be conserved and wisely used in the future

Table 1.2 Differences between conservation and restoration

	Conservation	*Restoration*
Planning strategy	Forecast planning and maintaining what is there (the baseline is the current state)	Back-cast planning (the baseline is set at a point in the past to match the aims of the project, although sometimes the final condition of the environment is not clearly described)
Goals	Environmental integrity; keeping the existing environment intact	Economic as well as environmental integrity: Not necessarily concerned with reinstating a former environment (retaining environment could be a secondary goal)
Socially constructed problem	Doesn't necessarily need a problem directly damaging human lives	Always needs a social 'problem' which impacts human lives and is solvable and good value for money
Geographical boundaries	Usually a defined area	Start with a defined area with a possibility of expansion in the future
Criticisms	'not providing income to society'	'creating an idealised past' 'using a baseline which not all environmentalists or ecologists agree upon'

In terms of project aims, conservation activities may or may not have a particular social problem to solve. In contrast, any restoration project needs socially constructed problems for humans to solve in order to secure funding. Although, what problems are perceived to be solvable and economically appropriate (value for money) is open for debate. The three restoration projects we will look at for this book had very clear socially constructed problems: in England, creating 'space for water' for sea-level rise and flood mitigation; in Malaysia, minimising the impact from tsunamis; and in Japan improving water quality in the ocean to support the fish and pearl industries. In restorations, economics plays as important a role as environmental integrity. Other differences between conservation and restoration are listed in Table 1.2.

In considering these differences between conservation and restoration, researchers of social perceptions have to be aware that citizens will see a project not only in terms of how important they feel the nature they are trying to reclaim is, but also its ideas and goals to evaluate the timeline and economic benefits, as well as the feasibilities of the restoration project itself.

1.6 The structure of the book

To ensure the strengths of the book are effectively expressed throughout the chapters, the structure of the rest of the book is designed as follows:

Chapter 2 ('Coastal wetland restoration in the world: Needs, challenges and benefits' by Rob McInnes) gives an overview of the tidal flat and coastal wetland restoration efforts in Europe, as well as other parts of the world. It also explains various environmental policies, including international agendas and initiatives that have been encouraging natural restoration initiatives, and the statistics related to the drive.

Chapter 3 ('To enable communities to engage with the biggest European tidal flat and saltmarsh restoration project' by Tim McGrath) is written by the restoration project manager himself. This chapter presents how five years of engaging and working closely with local communities led to the development of the largest coastal habitat creation in the UK. The author describes the background policy drivers and objectives behind the project, and the thought put into involving the local communities.

Chapter 4 ('People's perceptions towards the Steart Marshes creation project through stakeholder interviews and questionnaires' by Rob McInnes, Mark Everard and Hiromi Yamashita) then presents a more detailed analysis of the research interviews and questionnaires from the Steart Marshes project in Somerset, as outlined in Chapter 3. The on-the-ground data presents interesting differences between how the contractors explained the benefits of the project and how local people perceived them.

Chapter 5 ('Local power in a mangrove restoration project in Kuala Gula, Malaysia by Balu Perumal) shows on-the-ground experience of the Mangrove Rehabilitation Project in Kuala Gula, Malaysia. The chapter is written by the project manager who lived in the village for three years and shares some tips on communicating and meeting locals' needs as well as promoting a natural restoration project in a rural fishing village. Ten years later, achievements include the planting of more than 100,000 mangrove saplings in an area covering 100 ha of tidal flats.

Chapter 6 ('Kuala Gula research results' by Hiromi Yamashita and Naoyuki Mikami) then follows on to explore the interview and questionnaire results from the stakeholder villages in the Kuala Gula case study. The data reveals differing views towards the project among the various communities, which implies expanding the project would require a sophisticated approach to meet the diverse needs and perceptions.

Chapter 7 ('The Ago Bay experience from the local government viewpoint' by Hideto Uranaka) shares the viewpoint of the municipal government office and how they put a tidal flat restoration project on the city's agenda, when no such coastal realignment project had been done before in the country. The story is based in Shima City, previously known for its abundance of produce and famous for its offerings to the Imperial Court and Ise Grand Shrine.

Chapter 8 ('Creating the first tidal flat restoration project in Japan in Ago Bay' by Hideki Kokubu), written by the principle oceanography researcher from the prefectural government, explains the methods used for the tidal flat restoration project in Japan, which was the first to utilise unused farmland. It explains the ecological impacts the project had, explores current system barriers and how the project dealt with them.

Chapter 9 ('The Ago Bay tidal flat restoration project: Citizens' perceptions' by Naoyuki Mikami and Hiromi Yamashita) continues to share the interview and questionnaire results from the Ago Bay area, as presented in Chapter 8. The results show that the success indicators for the restoration project set by the citizens were very precise and different from those set by the local governmental officials.

Chapter 10 ('Challenges and opportunities for coastal wetlands: Restoration and community development' by Hiromi Yamashita and Naoyuki Mikami) summarises all the chapters and compares interview and questionnaire results from the three different case studies. Learning includes breaking down the myth of 'public disapproval' of restoration activities; local communities' reasoning for the activities; and how project promoters could engage with local people during and after a project.

This book shines light on coastal wetland restoration activities, not only on the ecological aspects but also the societal meaning, opportunities, social perceptions and future obstacles attached to them. It provides both academic research results and very rich data from the practitioners on the ground who have observed over long periods the difficulties and opportunities of such projects, as well as changes in local people's perceptions. These careful and considered attempts are also interesting in understanding what might be influential factors in citizens' perceptions towards restoration projects.

This book's Case Study Information Boxes and Appendices provide detailed information on the research activities, including information about each restoration site and the data collection and sampling methods of the questionnaire surveys. It is hoped that this book will be useful for both natural and social scientists who are involved in making decisions and policies, as well as those responsible for the day-to-day management of coastal or other types of ecological restoration.

References

Arnstein, S. R. (1969) 'A Ladder Of Citizen Participation.' *Journal of the American Institute of Planners*, 35(4), 216–224.

Curado, G., Manzano-Arrondo, V., Figueroa, E. and Castillo, J.M. (2014) 'Public perception and use of natural and restored salt marshes.' *Landscape Research*, 39(6), 668–679.

Davidson, N.C. (2014) 'How much wetland has the world lost?' *Marine and Freshwater Research*, 65(10), 936–941.

England, J., Skinner, K.S. and Carter, M.G. (2008) 'Monitoring, river restoration and the Water Framework Directive.' *Water and Environment Journal*, *22*(4), 227–234.

Environment Agency (2021) *Saltmarsh restoration handbook*. Bristol: Environment Agency.

Esteves, L. (2014) *Managed realignment: A viable long-term coastal management strategy?* Heidelberg: Springer Netherlands.

Esteves, L.S. and Thomas, K. (2014) 'Managed realignment in practice in the UK: Results from two independent surveys.' *Journal of Coastal Research,* 70, 407–413.

French, P.W. (2001) *Coastal defences: Processes, problems and solutions*. Abingdon-on-Thames: Psychology Press.

Goeldner-Gianella, L. (2007) 'Perception and attitudes toward de-polderisation in Europe: A comparison of five opinion surveys in France and the UK.' *Journal of Coastal Research*, 23(5), 1218–1230.

Gofman, J.W. (1981) *Radiation and human health*. London: Sierra Club Book.

Hart, R.A. (1992) *Children's participation: From tokenism to citizenship*. Florence: UNICEF Innocenti Centre.

Katz, S.B. and Miller, C.R. (1996) The low-level radioactive waste siting controversy in North Carolina: Toward a rhetorical model of risk communication. In: C. C. Herndl & S. B. Brown (Eds.), *Green culture: Environmental rhetoric in contemporary America* (pp. 111–140). Madison, WI: University of Wisconsin Press.

Luhmann, N. (1993) *Communication and social order: risk: A sociological theory*. Piscataway, NJ: Transaction Publishers.

Mitsch, W.J. (2010) 'Conservation, restoration and creation of wetlands: A global perspective.' In: Comin, F.A. (ed.), *Ecological restoration: A global challenge*. Cambridge: Cambridge University Press, pp. 175–187.

Myatt, L.B., Scrimshaw, M.D. and Lester, J.N. (2003a) 'Public perceptions and attitudes towards current managed realignment scheme: Brancaster West Marsh, North Norfolk, U.K.' *Journal of Coastal Research,* 19(2), 278–286.

Myatt, L.B., Scrimshaw, M.D. and Lester, J.N. (2003b) 'Public perceptions and attitudes towards a forthcoming managed realignment scheme: Freiston Shore, Lincolnshire, UK.' *Ocean & Coastal Management*, 46(6–7), 565–582.

Myatt, L.B., Scrimshaw, M.D. and Lester, J.N. (2003c) 'Public perceptions and attitudes towards an established managed realignment scheme: Orplands, Essex, UK.' *Journal of Environmental Management*, 68(2), 173–181.

Myatt-Bell, L.B., Scrimshaw, M.D., Lester, J.N. and Potts, J.S. (2002) 'Public perception of managed realignment: Brancaster West Marsh, North Norfolk, UK.' *Marine Policy*, 26(1), 45–57.

Oka, T. (1996) 'Risk and benefit analysis of environmental issues.' *Water Resources and Environment Research*, 9, 19–25 (in Japanese).

Pimbert, M.P., and Pretty, J.N. (1994) *Participation, people and the management of national parks and protected areas: Past failures and future promise*. UNRISD, IIED and WWF, mimeo.

Ramsar Convention Secretariat. (2018a) *Resolution XIII.20. Promoting the conservation and wise use of intertidal wetlands and ecologically-associated habitats*. Gland: Ramsar Convention Secretariat.

Ramsar Convention Secretariat. (2018b) *Global wetland outlook*. Gland: Ramsar Convention Secretariat.

Renn, O., Webler, T. and Wiedemann, P. (1995) 'A need for discourse on citizen participation: objectives and structure of the book.' In: Renn, O., Webler, T. and Wiedemann, P. (eds.) *Fairness and competence in citizen participation* (pp. 1–15). Dordrecht: Springer.

Roca, E. and Villares, M. (2012) 'Public perceptions of managed realignment strategies: The case study of the Ebro Delta in the Mediterranean basin.' *Ocean & Coastal Management*, 60, 38–47.

SER International Science and Policy Working Group (2004) The SER international primer on ecological restoration (version 2). Accessed October 27, 2020 at: https://www.ctahr.hawaii.edu/littonc/PDFs/682_SERPrimer.pdf

Terada, R. (2016) *Kankyo risk shakai no torai to kankyo undo* [Environmental risk society and environmental movement]. Tokyo (in Japanese): Meiji University.

Yamashita, H. (2015) 'Social perceptions on the risks and benefits of tidal flat restorations: Weakness identified in the past research literature.' *Proceedings of the 5th International Symposium on Environmental Sociology in East Asia*, pp. 289–298.

2 Coastal wetland restoration in the world

Needs, challenges and benefits

Robert J. McInnes

2.1 Coastal wetlands: Status and trends

2.1.1 Current extent of coastal and tidal wetlands

Coastal and tidal wetlands occur at the interface of the land and the sea (Scott et al., 2014). Article 1.1 of the Ramsar Convention text defines wetlands as "areas of marsh, fen, peatland or water, whether natural or artificial, permanent or temporary, with water that is static or flowing, fresh, brackish or salt, including areas of marine water the depth of which at low tide does not exceed six metres" (Ramsar Convention, 1971, p. 2). Therefore, coastal and tidal wetlands represent diverse and dynamic ecosystems. Under the Ramsar Convention's typology of wetlands, saline or brackish water coastal wetlands are categorised into five groups: permanent, shores, intertidal, lagoons and estuarine waters. Permanent wetlands include coral reefs and seagrass beds, and shores include rocky, sandy or shingle coasts. Intertidal wetlands are further classified as flats (mud, sand or salt), marshes (saltmarshes) and forested (mangroves). In addition, the Ramsar Convention recognises that freshwater lagoons and subterranean wetlands may be present in the coastal environment (Ramsar Convention Secretariat, 2010).

Davidson and Finlayson (2018) estimated the global extent of marine/coastal wetlands to be a minimum of 1.64×10^6 km^2. However, insufficient data are available to generate reliable estimates of the global, spatial extent of sand dunes, beaches and rocky shores, shellfish reefs, kelp forests, shallow subtidal marine systems and coastal karst and caves. Unvegetated tidal flats (0.458×10^6 km^2) and saltmarshes (0.550×10^6 km^2) account for more than 60% of the global coastal wetland area. These coastal wetland systems are not evenly distributed around the world. It has been estimated that more than two-thirds of the global extent of tidal flats are recorded in three continents (Asia (44%); North

DOI: 10.4324/9780367863098-2

America (15.5%); and South America (11%)). Furthermore, almost half of the world's tidal flats are concentrated in just eight countries (Indonesia, China, Australia, the United States, Canada, India, Brazil and Myanmar) (Murray et al., 2019). Similarly, an uneven distribution is observed for saltmarshes with more than two-fifths of the global resource concentrated around the coast of North America (41% of the global area) and a further two-fifths split between Oceania (25%) and Europe (21%) (Davidson and Finlayson, 2018).

2.1.2 *Current rates of coastal wetland degradation and loss*

Globally, wetlands are under threat from degradation and loss, with estimates suggesting that the world may have lost 87% of its wetlands since 1700 CE (Davidson, 2014). There is evidence that rates of wetland loss have accelerated since the beginning of the twentieth century, with coastal wetland loss estimated to be 4.2 times faster since 1900 than over the long term (Davidson, 2014). This decline in coastal wetlands is distributed across all wetland types (Davidson and Finlayson, 2018).

For areas of the world where robust data exist, it has been estimated that more than 16% of the global extent of tidal flats have been lost in the 32 years between 1984 and 2016 (Murray et al., 2019). In some regions, the loss percentages are substantially higher. Li et al. (2018) estimated that 73% of coastal wetlands around Bohai Bay, China, were lost between 2000 and 2010. More widely in the same region, Murray et al. (2014) estimated that 65% of the tidal flats surrounding the Yellow Sea have been lost since the middle of the twentieth century. A review of the status of European coastal wetlands indicated that Greece has lost 73% of all its saltmarshes since 1900, Denmark has lost 60% of all its coastal wetlands since 1870 and in France 86% of coastal and tidal wetlands have been lost during the twentieth century (Airoldi and Beck, 2007).

2.1.3 *Drivers of coastal wetland degradation and loss*

Coastal wetlands around the world are being lost and degraded through human activities. In some places this has resulted in the wholesale loss of wetlands, such as through the construction of a 33 km-long sea wall and subsequent draining and reclamation of some 400 km^2 of tidal flats around Saemangeum in the Republic of Korea (Lie et al., 2008). In other parts of the world, coastal wetlands remain but their physical properties and ecological communities have become severely degraded. Sometimes natural coastal wetlands are subject to wholesale transformation and conversion into different ecosystems. The expansion of commercial shrimp aquaculture in Puttalam lagoon, Sri Lanka, has resulted in the area of shrimp farms increasing by 2,777%, mainly at the expense of mangroves. Due to problems with disease, approximately 90% of these shrimp farms were abandoned within a few years, leaving a denuded and unproductive coastal landscape (Bournazel et al., 2015). Globally, chronic challenges such as pollution, reductions in sediment supply, invasive species, human disturbance and over-exploitation, or acute events such as oil spills or severe storms, progressively degrade the remaining coastal wetlands.

There is abundant evidence that chronic impacts can degrade the ecology of coastal wetlands (Spencer et al., 2016; Murray et al., 2019). For instance, the saltmarshes of the Tagus Estuary, Portugal have experienced significant accumulation of anthropogenic-sourced heavy metals, as a result of direct discharges from industry and urban areas; these are bioaccumulating in benthic invertebrates and generating negative consequences at different trophic levels in the estuarine food web (França et al., 2005). In northern Spain, the 1,200 ha of intertidal marshes of the Santoña, Victoria and Joyel Marshes Natural Park regularly support over 20,000 wintering waterbirds. The introduction of recreational activities, such as walking, into this previously undisturbed coastal environment has demonstrated a systematic increase in the daily energy expenditure of shorebirds, causing physiological stress at an individual level, and in some cases causing birds to avoid the site completely, affecting the overall population dynamics (Navedo and Herrera, 2012). Dams, catchment land use changes and alteration to other riverine processes can have serious implications for sediment supply to the coastal zone. The Nile Delta has experienced a 98% reduction in sediment supply since the beginning of the twentieth century (Syvitski et al., 2009), which, when coupled with sea-level rise, beach erosion and land subsidence (Frihy et al., 2010), is having a serious impact on the low-lying coastal wetlands.

Sea-level rise can be considered a threat to coastal wetlands; however, there is a school of thought that wetlands can migrate landwards if they are not constrained by a sea wall, uplands or other physical barriers, such as anthropogenic infrastructure (Li et al., 2018). Both direct and indirect biotic processes are likely to have a significant influence on the ability of coastal marshes to adjust to sea-level rise, particularly whether marsh surface accretion can keep pace with rising sea levels (Cahoon et al., 2006). Modelling studies have confirmed that wetlands subject to a micro-tidal regime are likely to have a greater vulnerability to future loss than those in macro-tidal environments. Addressing the potential loss of coastal wetlands will necessitate both a global response to climate mitigation to combat sea-level rise and the provision of suitable space for migration and sediment supply to low-lying coastal environments (Spencer et al., 2016).

2.1.4 Where does restoration fit in addressing the current status and trends of coastal wetlands?

The restoration of coastal and tidal wetlands has a significant history. Some 50 years ago, Gagliano et al. (1970) highlighted the need and response options to address wetland loss in the Mississippi Delta. Moving forward almost half a century, the importance of restoring coastal wetlands forms a critical component of the international and local response to the declining status and extent of wetlands. In 2018, the Ramsar Convention published the report 'Global Wetland Outlook: State of the World's Wetlands and their Services to People' (Ramsar Convention on Wetlands, 2018), highlighting the need for governments around the world to fund and support wetland restoration as a strategic response to ongoing wetland degradation and loss. Resolution XII.2 established the 4th Strategic Plan 2016–2024 for the Ramsar Convention (Ramsar Convention, 2015). The importance of wetland restoration is firmly established through Goal 3, Target 12 of the Strategic Plan, which states that, "restoration is in progress in degraded wetlands, with priority to wetlands that are relevant for biodiversity conservation, disaster risk reduction, livelihoods and/or climate change mitigation and adaptation". The significance of restoring coastal wetlands is also embedded in Goal 6.6 of the United Nations' Sustainable Development Goals (SDGs) through the ambition "to protect and restore water-related ecosystems, including mountains, forests, wetlands, rivers, aquifers and lakes". These global initiatives provide an overriding context for promoting and pursuing the restoration of coastal wetlands. However, while it is apt to 'think globally', it is essential that the scalar challenges to sustainable development and restoring lost and degraded coastal wetlands embrace the need to 'act locally' (Stratford, 2004).

2.2 Restoration benefits and challenges

2.2.1 The relevance and benefits of coastal wetland restoration initiatives

Tidal and coastal wetland restoration forms part of an essential strategy aimed at stemming the degradation and loss of wetlands, a key component of climate change mitigation and adaptation strategies (Ramsar Convention on Wetlands, 2018). Under a changing and increasingly variable climate, traditional approaches to coastal protection and management have begun to shift away from the hard-engineered concept of 'holding the line' to more flexible and adaptive approaches, which combine 'soft-engineering' or 'natural infrastructure' (Esteves, 2014). For tidal wetland restoration to be strategic within this new coastal management paradigm shift, understanding of the relevant physical, ecological and social processes must continually be improved. Further research is required to enhance the predictability of outcomes (both biophysically and socio-economically), as well as the time frame required for ecosystem recovery and the relevance of adaptive management strategies (Goodwin et al., 2001).

Globally, calls have been made for coastal wetland restoration as a cost-effective, sustainable and socio-ecologically sound approach to rising sea levels, increased storm intensity and flooding of coastal communities (Temmerman et al., 2013). These calls have resulted in the implementation of restoration initiatives across the world. Some initiatives are a direct response to a catastrophic event, such as the evolving efforts to restore the wetlands in the Mississippi Deltaic Plan post Hurricane Katrina (Day et al., 2007) or recognition of the need to protect and restore mangrove ecosystems to mitigate against storm surges and minor tsunamis in the wake of the Indian Ocean Tsunami in 2004 (Larsen et al., 2008; Marois and Mitsch, 2015). Other attempts form vital components of a strategic shift towards more viable, long-term management of the coastal zone (Esteves, 2014).

Many coastal wetland restoration initiatives form part of a pro-active rather than reactive agenda, aimed at delivering more sustainable outcomes within the coastal zone. Usually, active approaches are accomplished through 'engineered' actions that intentionally attempt to recreate lost or degraded wetland structures and processes (Simenstad et al., 2006). For instance, in Belgium 2,500 ha of historically reclaimed wetlands are being restored to tidal marshes in the Sigma Plan as part of a wider, strategic approach to reduce the socio-economic impacts of flooding from the tidal Scheldt River (De Vlaamse Waterweg nv and Natuur en Bos, 2020; Broekx et al., 2011). The project should be completed by 2030 with an expected cost of €600 million, which can be set against a yearly risk of flood damage estimated at €1 billion by 2100. This demonstrates the need to combine natural infrastructure solutions through the restoration of tidal marshes and flats with more traditional 'engineered' solutions to deliver the optimal cost solution (Broekx et al., 2011).

Increasingly, the multi-functional role of coastal wetlands is being recognised (McInnes, 2011). The management and restoration of seagrasses, mangroves, saltmarshes and tidal flats is being advocated as a response to increased sea-level rise and the associated impacts from storm surges and flooding, as well as their critical role in sequestering and storing carbon. Even within highly urbanised landscapes, the restoration of tidal wetlands can deliver multiple, strategic benefits. For instance, Jamaica Bay is located within the Boroughs of Brooklyn and Queens in New York City. The estuarine system has suffered a range of impacts from significant urban and industrial development, resulting in large-scale habitat loss and conversion (Hartig et al., 2002). Restoration of Jamaica Bay's saltmarshes and tidal flats began in 2003. The restoration activities have been successful in stemming habitat loss (Campbell et al., 2017) and have contributed to the delivery of a wider range of benefits such as reducing the impacts of storm surges, enhancing the area as a fish nursery, providing a secure habitat for roosting and breeding birds, and offering recreational and environmental educational opportunities for visitors (Campbell et al., 2015).

2.2.2 Contributions to global agendas

The Ramsar Convention on Wetlands (2018) recognises the crucial role that wetland restoration can play in the delivery of the global sustainability agenda. As has been highlighted, tidal wetland restoration can support the implementation of Sustainable Development Goals (SDGs) along with strategic objectives of multi-lateral environmental agreements (MEAs). Opportunities also exist for the outcomes of restoration activities to be included in developing countries' National Appropriate Mitigation Actions (NAMAs) in the context of sustainable development and reducing emissions (Crooks et al., 2011), and as important elements in Nationally Determined Contributions (NDCs) under Article 4 of the Paris Agreement within the United Nations Framework Convention on Climate Change (Herr and Landis, 2016). Similarly, tidal wetland restoration can play a critical and strategic role in contributing to other inter-governmental processes such as the Sendai Framework for Disaster Risk Reduction (Kumar et al., 2017).

2.2.3 Why is coastal wetland restoration not being more widely implemented?

If the restoration of coastal wetlands represents a cost-effective, multiple benefit outcome, why are initiatives not more widespread or mainstream? Simenstad et al. (2006) argue that to be ecologically functional and self-sustaining, wetland restoration requires understanding and reinstating fundamental ecosystem processes from site to landscape scales. Sometimes the focus remains on the site and not on the wider landscape (which can consider not just environmental but also social, governance and political landscapes), or even more myopically on vegetation responses or numbers of breeding birds (Zhao et al., 2016). Methodological challenges also act as barriers to fully integrate the ecosystem services and wider values of the restoration of natural infrastructure at both a policy and site design level (Iacob et al., 2012), and on how to evaluate restoration 'success' (Zhao et al., 2016). In addition, there remain public perception barriers regarding the risks of sustainability (Myatt et al., 2003) and potential conflicts of interest (Roca and Villares, 2012).

2.3 Conclusion

In the face of unremitting and progressive loss of coastal wetlands, and against the backdrop of global sustainability agendas, there is a strong case for restoration of these threatened ecosystems. Decisions need to be evidence based and inclusive in order to convince policy makers and local communities alike that coastal wetland restoration represents a genuine systemic solution (Everard and McInnes, 2013), which can connect wide networks of interests to deliver mutually beneficial outcomes for society.

References

Airoldi, L. and Beck, M.W. (2007) 'Loss, status and trends for coastal marine habitats of Europe.' *Oceanography and Marine Biology: An Annual Review*, 45, 345–405.

Bournazel, J., Kumara, M.P., Jayatissa, L.P., Viergever, K., Morel, V. and Huxham, M. (2015) 'The impacts of shrimp farming on land-use and carbon storage around Puttalam lagoon, Sri Lanka.' *Ocean & Coastal Management*, 113, 18–28.

Broekx, S., Smets, S., Liekens, I., Bulckaen, D. and De Nocker, L. (2011) 'Designing a long-term flood risk management plan for the Scheldt estuary using a risk-based approach.' *Natural Hazards*, 57(2), 245–266.

Cahoon, D.R., Hensel, P.F., Spencer, T., Reed, D.J., McKee, K.L. and Saintilan, N. (2006) 'Coastal wetland vulnerability to relative sea-level rise: wetland elevation trends and process controls.' In: Verhoeven, J.T.A., Beltman, B., Bobbink, R. and Whigham, D.F. (eds.), *Wetlands and natural resource management.* Berlin: Springer, pp. 271–292.

Campbell, L., Svendsen, E., Sonti, N. and Johnson, M. (2015) *Reading the landscape: A social assessment of parks and their natural areas in Jamaica Bay communities.* White Paper, Part I: Social Assessment Overview. Queens, NY: US Forest Service, New York City Urban Field Station.

Campbell, A., Wang, Y., Christiano, M. and Stevens, S. (2017) 'Salt marsh monitoring in Jamaica Bay, New York from 2003 to 2013: A decade of change from restoration to Hurricane Sandy.' *Remote Sensing*, 9(2), 131.

Crooks, S., Herr, D., Tamelander, J., Laffoley, D. and Vandever, J. (2011) *Mitigating climate change through restoration and management of coastal wetlands and near-shore marine ecosystems: Challenges and opportunities.* Environment Department Paper 121. Washington, DC: World Bank.

Davidson, N.C. (2014) How much wetland has the world lost? Long-term and recent trends in global wetland area. *Marine and Freshwater Research*, 65(10), 934-941.

Davidson, N.C. and Finlayson, C.M. (2018) Extent, regional distribution and changes in area of different classes of wetland. *Marine and Freshwater Research*, 69(10), 1525–1533.

Day, J.W., Boesch, D.F., Clairain, E.J., Kemp, G.P., Laska, S.B., Mitsch, W.J., ... and Simenstad, C. A. (2007) 'Restoration of the Mississippi Delta: Lessons from hurricanes Katrina and Rita.' *Science*, 315(5819), 1679–1684.

De Vlaamse Waterweg nv and Natuur en Bos (2020 online) *What is the Sigma Plan?* Antwerp: De Vlaamse Waterweg nv and Natuur en Bos (Agency for Nature and Forests), Accessed October 27, 2020 at https://www.sigmaplan.be/en/

Esteves, L. (2014) (ed.) *Managed realignment: A viable long-term coastal management strategy?* Dordrech: Springer.

Esteves, L.S. (2014) 'The need for adaptation in coastal protection: Shifting from hard engineering to managed realignment.' In: Esteves, L.S. (ed.), *Managed realignment: A viable long-term coastal management strategy?* Dordrecht: Springer, pp. 1–18.

Everard, M. and McInnes, R. (2013) Systemic solutions for multi-benefit water and environmental management. *Science of the Total Environment*, 461, 170–179.

França, S., Vinagre, C., Caçador, I. and Cabral, H.N. (2005) 'Heavy metal concentrations in sediment, benthic invertebrates and fish in three salt marsh areas subjected to different pollution loads in the Tagus Estuary (Portugal).' *Marine Pollution Bulletin*, 50(9), 998–1003.

Frihy, O.E.S., Deabes, E.A., Shereet, S.M. and Abdalla, F.A. (2010) 'Alexandria-Nile Delta coast, Egypt: Update and future projection of relative sea-level rise.' *Environmental Earth Sciences*, 61(2), 253–273.

Gagliano, S.M., Kwon, H.J. and Van Beek, J.L. (1970) 'Deterioration and restoration of coastal wetlands.' *Coastal Engineering Proceedings* 1(12), 1767–1781.

Goodwin, P., Mehta, A.J. and Zedler, J.B. (2001) 'Tidal wetland restoration: An introduction.' *Journal of Coastal Research Special Issue*, 27, 1–6.

Hartig, E.K., Gornitz, V., Kolker, A., Mushacke, F. and Fallon, D. (2002) Anthropogenic and climate-change impacts on salt marshes of Jamaica Bay, New York City. *Wetlands*, 22(1), 71–89.

Herr, D. and Landis, E. (2016) *Coastal blue carbon ecosystems: Opportunities for nationally determined contributions. Policy brief.* Gland, Switzerland: IUCN; Washington, DC: TNC.

Iacob, O., Rowan, J., Brown, I. and Ellis, C. (2012). *Natural flood management as a climate change adaptation option assessed using an ecosystem services approach*. Paper presented at BHS Eleventh National Hydrology Symposium, Dundee, United Kingdom. https://doi.org/10.7558/bhs.2012.ns26

Kumar, R., Tol, S., McInnes, R.J., Everard, M. and Kulindwa, A.A. (2017) *Wetlands for disaster risk reduction: Effective choices for resilient communities*. Ramsar Policy Brief No. 1. Gland, Switzerland: Ramsar Convention Secretariat.

Larsen, R.K., Miller, F. and Thomalla, F. (2008) *Vulnerability in the context of post 2004 Indian Ocean tsunami recovery: Lessons for building more resilient coastal communities. A synthesis of documented factors contributing to tsunami related vulnerability in Sri Lanka and Indonesia*. Risks, Livelihoods and Vulnerability Programme: Working paper. Stockholm, Sweden: Stockholm Environment Institute.

Li, X., Bellerby, R., Craft, C. and Widney, S.E. (2018) 'Coastal wetland loss, consequences, and challenges for restoration.' *Anthropocene Coasts*, 1(1), 1–15.

Lie, H.J., Cho, C.H., Lee, S., Kim, E.S., Koo, B.J. and Noh, J.H. (2008) 'Changes in marine environment by a large coastal development of the Saemangeum reclamation project in Korea.' *Ocean and Polar Research*, 30(4), 475–484.

Marois, D.E. and Mitsch, W.J. (2015) 'Coastal protection from tsunamis and cyclones provided by mangrove wetlands: A review.' *International Journal of Biodiversity Science, Ecosystem Services & Management*, 11(1), 71–83.

McInnes, R.J. (2011) 'Managing wetlands for multifunctional benefits.' In: Le Page, B. (ed.), *Wetlands.* Dordrecht: Springer, 205–221.

Murray, N.J., Clemens, R.S., Phinn, S.R., Possingham, H.P. and Fuller, R.A. (2014) 'Tracking the rapid loss of tidal wetlands in the Yellow Sea.' *Frontiers in Ecology and the Environment*, 12(5), 267–272.

Murray, N.J., Phinn, S.R., DeWitt, M., Ferrari, R., Johnston, R., Lyons, M. B., ... and Fuller, R.A. (2019) 'The global distribution and trajectory of tidal flats.' *Nature*, 565(7738), 222–225.

Myatt, L.B., Scrimshaw, M.D. and Lester, J.N. (2003) 'Public perceptions and attitudes towards a current managed realignment scheme: Brancaster West Marsh, North Norfolk, UK.' *Journal of Coastal Research*, 19(2), 278–286.

Navedo, J.G. and Herrera, A.G. (2012) 'Effects of recreational disturbance on tidal wetlands: Supporting the importance of undisturbed roosting sites for waterbird conservation.' *Journal of Coastal Conservation*, 16(3), 373–381.

Ramsar Convention (1971) *The Convention on Wetlands text, as originally adopted in 1971*. Accessed June 10, 2020 at https://www.ramsar.org/document/present-text-of-the-convention-on-wetlands

Ramsar Convention (2015) *The 4th Strategic Plan 2016-2024*. Resolution Xii.2 adopted by the 12th Meeting of the Conference of the Parties at Punta del Este, Uruguay, 1-9 June 2015. Accessed 10 June 2020 at https://www.ramsar.org/document/the-fourth-ramsar-strategic-plan-2016-2024

Ramsar Convention on Wetlands (2018) *Global wetland outlook: State of the world's wetlands and their services to people*. Gland, Switzerland: Ramsar Convention Secretariat, p. 88.

Ramsar Convention Secretariat (2010) *Designating Ramsar sites: Strategic framework and guidelines for the future development of the List of Wetlands of International Importance, Ramsar handbooks for the wise use of wetlands, 4th edition, vol. 17*. Gland, Switzerland: Ramsar Convention Secretariat.

Roca, E. and Villares, M. (2012) 'Public perceptions of managed realignment strategies: The case study of the Ebro Delta in the Mediterranean basin.' *Ocean & Coastal Management*, 60, 38–47.

Scott, D.B., Frail-Gauthier, J. and Mudie, P.J. (2014) *Coastal wetlands of the world: Geology, ecology, distribution and applications*. Cambridge: Cambridge University Press.

Simenstad, C., Reed, D. and Ford, M. (2006) 'When is restoration not?: Incorporating landscape-scale processes to restore self-sustaining ecosystems in coastal wetland restoration.' *Ecological Engineering*, 26(1), 27–39.

Spencer, T., Schuerch, M., Nicholls, R.J., Hinkel, J., Lincke, D., Vafeidis, A.T., ... and Brown, S. (2016) 'Global coastal wetland change under sea-level rise and related stresses: The DIVA Wetland Change Model.' *Global and Planetary Change*, 139, 15–30.

Stratford, E. (2004) 'Think global, act local: Scalar challenges to sustainable development of marine environments.' In: White, R. (ed.), *Controversies in environmental sociology*. New York: Cambridge University Press, pp. 150–167.

Syvitski, J.P., Kettner, A.J., Overeem, I., Hutton, E.W., Hannon, M.T., Brakenridge, G.R., ... and Nicholls, R.J. (2009) 'Sinking deltas due to human activities.' *Nature Geoscience*, 2(10), 681–686.

Temmerman, S., Meire, P., Bouma, T.J., Herman, P.M., Ysebaert, T. and De Vriend, H.J. (2013) 'Ecosystem-based coastal defence in the face of global change.' *Nature*, 504(7478), 79–83.

Zhao, Q., Bai, J., Huang, L., Gu, B., Lu, Q. and Gao, Z. (2016) 'A review of methodologies and success indicators for coastal wetland restoration.' *Ecological Indicators*, 60, 442–452.

Case Study A information for Chapters 3 and 4

The Steart Coastal Managed Realignment Project, Steart Peninsula, Bridgwater, Somerset, UK

Tim McGrath, Robert J. McInnes, and Hiromi Yamashita

The project made direct links between global (climate change) and regional agendas (looking for saltmarsh mitigation sites) with local wants (a stronger flood defence). Thorough and detailed sets of consultation procedures enabled the community members to come together to embrace a significant change in their local area, and plan for the future with the project contractors. This project gives numerous examples of how decision-making mechanisms and the contractors responded to local concerns to enhance the site for both locals and visitors (e.g. path design, placing the car park strategically to stop visitors going into the village) (Table A.1).

Area background

The Steart peninsula covers some 1,000 ha between the mouth of the tidal River Parrett and the Bristol Channel in north Somerset, UK. The peninsula primarily comprises agricultural land, much of which occupies land below mean high water spring tide level. The village of Steart lies to the northern end of the peninsula and is connected to the mainland villages by road. The market town of Bridgwater lies some 9 km to the south. Historically, the peninsula has been protected from coastal flooding from the north by a natural shingle ridge at higher elevation than surrounding land, occasionally maintained and reinforced by bulldozing, and to the south and east by a continuous earth embankment (Figure A.1).

Estimates indicate that over the next 100 years between 1,500 and 3,500 ha of intertidal habitats will be lost due to coastal squeeze within the Severn Estuary and Bristol Channel area (Environment Agency, 2011). Much of this area is designated under European regulations for

Table A.1 Background information on the Steart Marshes Management Project

Site name	*Steart Marshes Management Project*
Location	Steart Peninsula, Bridgwater, Somerset, UK
Project type	Managed realignment
Year implemented	Discussion started 2008; breached the dyke on 5 September 2014
Size (ha)	400
Habitat(s) restored	Saltmarshes, tidal flats, freshwater wetlands
Aim of the project	Mitigating effects of the nearby port development on mudflats (Bristol Port), creating sites for migratory birds, building new sea walls for local community
Project contractor(s)	NGO and national government
Previous landowner(s)	Farmers
Stakeholders	Residents, farmers, landowners, local and national government, national NGO
Number of communities within the constituency	4 (Steart (community on the peninsula); Stockland Bristol; Otterhampton; Combwich)
Population	996 people (estimated by the District Council Office, 2018)

its importance as wildlife habitat and as such the UK government is obligated to provide compensatory habitat for such losses. Additionally, the local Shoreline Management Plan (SMP) promotes management policies with the long-term objectives of being technically sustainable, environmentally acceptable and economically viable. However, the economic case for maintaining the differences in the current condition failed to meet national funding guidelines. Therefore, to deliver on these policy objectives for the coastal section around the Steart Peninsula in the short term, the plan was to continue to minimise flood and erosion risk through managed realignment and, on the seaward side to hold the line, while in the medium to long term to move towards no active intervention (Halcrow, 2010). The dual drivers behind the scheme were the need to meet statutory nature conservation objectives through the provision of compensatory habitat creation and to comply with the economic drivers behind the policy objectives of the section of coastline.

Project summary

In the UK, interest in managed realignment began in the late 1980s, with the first projects initiated in the mid to late 1990s (Atkinson et al., 2004). In 2005, the UK government published *Making Space for Water*, and the primary aim of the strategy was to "reduce the threat to people and their property" and "deliver the greatest environmental, social and economic benefits" (Defra, 2005). The two main drivers behind the strategy were climate change adaptation and the statutory duty of nature conservation (principally Natura 2000) sites.

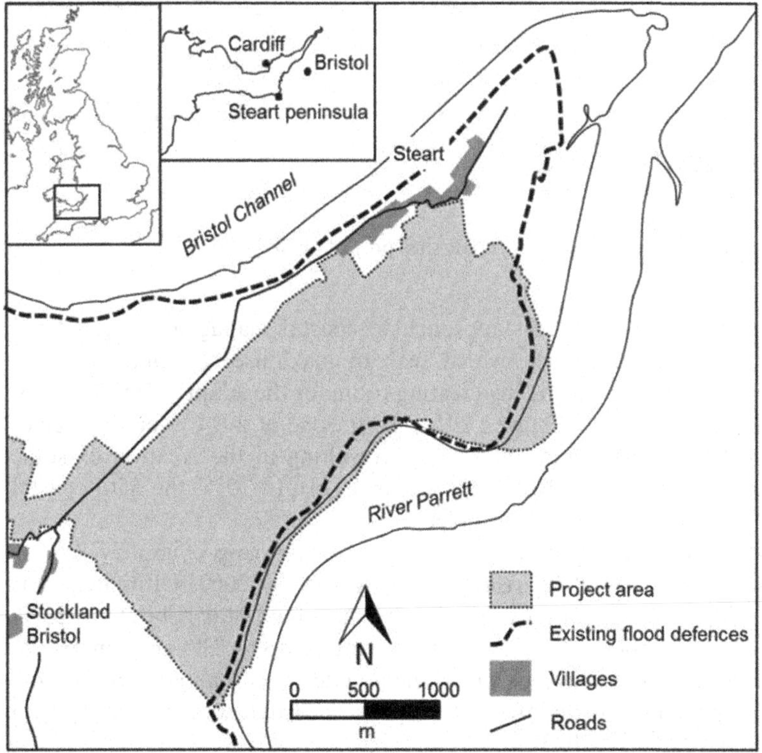

Figure A.1 Map of the Steart peninsula and the project area.

The project area is in the west part of Britain, close to Bristol. The 4 villages on and near the Steart Peninsula are indicated.

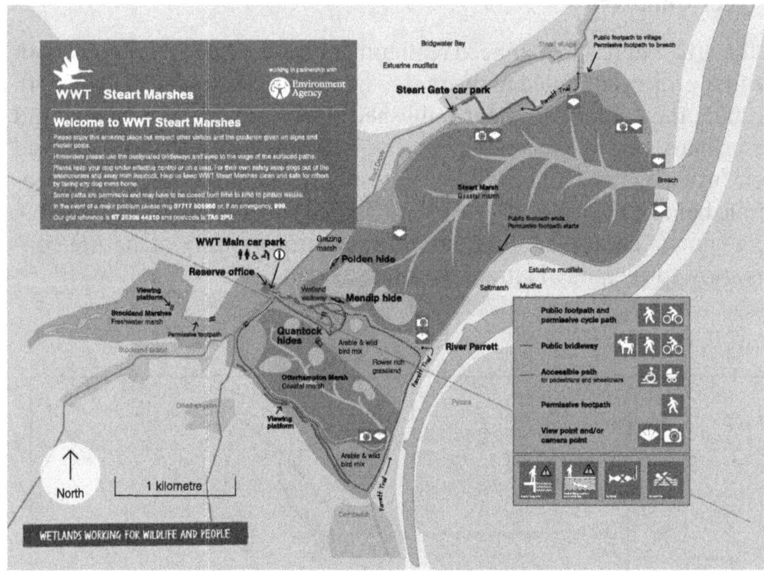

Figure A.2 Map of the Steart Marshes project (WWT, 2014).

This relatively recent approach to coastal management uses 'soft' engineering techniques, which seek to maximise environmental and socio-economic benefits by creating room for the adaptive development of coastal habitats (Esteves, 2014). By the end of 2014, over 50 schemes had been implemented in the UK, resulting in the creation of some 900 ha of intertidal habitat (Thomas, 2014). In 2017, the 55th coastal realignment project was completed.

The long-term plan in England is to realign approximately 10% of the coastline by 2030, rising to nearly 15% by 2060. Ultimately, this would involve creating around 6,200 ha of coastal habitat by 2030, rising to 11,500 ha by 2060, with a saving of up to £380 million in capital and maintenance costs over the long term, compared with the cost of replacing and maintaining existing hard defences (Committee on Climate Change, 2013).

Early discussions were held during 2002 and 2003 to engage the local community and stakeholders in considering the options for managing flood risk. In developing the final scheme, the Environment Agency (EA) assigned dedicated officers to undertake the consultation process and to act as focal points for local stakeholders (Figures A.2 and A.3).

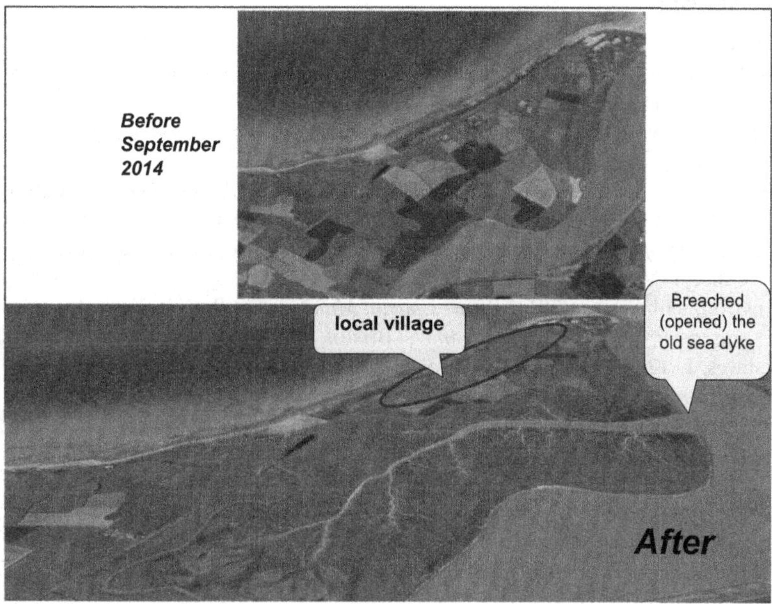

Figure A.3 Aerial photographs before and after the restoration project on the Steart Peninsula (WWT, 2014).

A planning application for the works was submitted by the EA to the local authority in December 2011 and permission was granted in March 2012; earthworks commenced in May 2012. The final submitted scheme proposed the following benefits:

- Creation of new areas of wetland including 194 ha of intertidal saltmarsh, 67 ha of transitional brackish habitat, 106 ha of coastal grazing marsh, 17 ha of brackish and saline lagoons, 8 ha of fresh-water lagoon, 12 ha of reed bed and numerous ponds and ditches.
- Provision of new habitats which will benefit plant diversity, breeding and wintering wading birds, wintering wildfowl, amphibians and fish.
- Improved flood risk management to properties and infrastructure.
- Creation of a valuable new recreational amenity and ecotourism destination.
- Construction of a low-key visitor attraction with limited facilities including toilets, interpretation boards, plants and fish.

References

Atkinson, P. W., Crooks, S., Drewitt, A., Grant, A., Rehfisch, M. M., Sharpe, J., and Tyas, C.J. (2004) 'Managed realignment in the UK-the first 5 years of colonization by birds.' *Ibis,* 146(1),101–110.

Committee on Climate Change (2013) *Managing the land in a changing climate.* London: The CCCuk.

Department of the Environment, Food and Rural Affairs (Defra) (2005) *Making space for water: Taking forward a new government strategy for flood and coastal erosion risk management in England.* London: The Stationery Office, HM Government.

Environment Agency (2011) *Steart Coastal Management Project: Environmental statement – Non-technical summary.* Bristol, UK: Environment Agency.

Esteves, L. (2014) (ed.) *Managed realignment: A viable long-term coastal management strategy?* Dordrech: Springer.

Halcrow (2010) *Shoreline Management Plan Review (SMP2) Hartland Point to Anchor Head, s.l.* Somerset: North Devon and Somerset Coastal Advisory Group.

Thomas, K. (2014) 'Managed realignment in the UK: The role of the Environment Agency.' In: Esteves, L.S. (ed.), *Managed realignment: Is it a viable long-term coastal management strategy?* Dordrecht: Springer.

3 To enable communities to engage with the biggest European tidal flat and saltmarsh restoration project

Tim McGrath

3.1 Background to the project site

The coastal communities around the Steart Peninsula in Bridgwater Bay lie within or on the edge of a flat coastal plain, the landscape of which has taken form through both the influence of man-made and natural processes. Agricultural management, the predominant land practice, began rapidly after land was reclaimed from the sea over 2,000 years ago (Wessex Archaeology, 2010). In the subsequent years, this business became the dominant driving force that shaped the fabric of the Steart Peninsula. Over time, this became more efficient through enforcing control over natural processes by increasing freshwater drainage and constructing ever-higher flood defences that reduced the risk of tidal flooding. Consequently, there has been, over hundreds of years, an acceptance that the landscape should always be agriculturally managed, and this approach became rooted in local culture. In addition, being surrounded by a landscape that remained stable and safe gave a positive reason for people to want to live there. On a lane that ends in a cul-de-sac, there is a clear sense of why such a remote and tranquil landscape is a good place to be.

However, natural processes working on a far greater scale than those applied to the landscape at Steart have a constant and significant effect on any artificial process trying to halt or reverse them (Atkins, 2013). Though perceived to be negligible (and even inconsequential) on a day-to-day basis, trying to keep these under control results in substantial investment in resources. An example of this is long-shore drift, a tidal process where marine sediment carried along the coastline with the prevailing tide shapes the landform of the peninsula, creating land for colonisation (Allen et al., 1998). It can also, by its very nature, remove sediment and over time weaken coastal defences, either natural or man-made, with an indirect effect of sudden and catastrophic incursion

DOI: 10.4324/9780367863098-3

of the tide and the high risk that flooding brings to property and life. Resisting this natural force is ultimately unsustainable and adapting to it requires long-term planning and making often somewhat controversial decisions (Adam , 2002).

In this context, allowing the tide to reclaim land after over 2,000 years of not experiencing natural tidal inundation went against the cultural grain that had developed. However, unexpected events, such as the failure of a flood bank during a storm surge in 1981, brought a new level of uncertainty to a landscape that had been previously thought defendable, and at this point doubt on the sustainability of anthropogenic management began (Pethick, 2002). The effect of rapid or forced change on people who have a stake in an environment can be challenging to accept. It is because of this, communities around the UK coastline at risk of such catastrophic change need to be aware of the risks and actively encouraged to participate in determining and agreeing a long-term solution (Defra/Environment Agency 2010). Investing in the right communication techniques will result in people feeling that they are better informed and have been listened to. Understanding and respecting this, alongside the background of why people value the space they occupy, is a vital cornerstone to applying the correct engagement tools that can eventually lead to an acceptance of any coastal change (Black and Veatch, 2009).

3.2 Engagement in the early stage

3.2.1 The importance of early involvement of local people

In September 2009, the Wildfowl & Wetlands Trust (WWT) was appointed by the Environment Agency (EA) as the future site management organisation and became a member of the Steart Coastal Management Project Team. It brought with it the knowledge and experience of how to engage people with wetlands. Its heritage and business style of putting people at the heart of decision making brought an attachment to understanding what people valued when experiencing wetlands. It is critical not to underestimate the time required to properly engage with people and ensure there are enough financial resources to provide a member of staff who is trusted and respected by the local community (Humber Community Project, 2008).

It is vital to recognise this is not a nine-to-five job, as engagement happens at any time of the day, and being available to respond to community requests is essential (Environment Agency, 2007). It is also important to ensure the right person is appointed to the role and that they have both the correct communication skills and an ability to clearly use language that local people understand. While it is not always possible, being able to appoint someone who is from the local area helps with understanding geography or knowing who local people are. Treating others how you would like to be treated yourself leads to an honest and open communication style; being courteous, friendly and respectful will lead to a long-lasting and trusting relationship. It is essential to carry out what you agree to do in any meeting and promptly follow it up with a response, and always be available to meet face to face to explain how the outcome was reached, especially if it was not the one that was expected.

At this early stage, clearly explain the course of what will happen, the timeline and the formal process of consultation, especially dates of any public meetings and key dates to respond by (Environment Agency, 2010). Also, it is important to explain the roles of Project Team members and give an opportunity for local people to get to know and meet key members of the team with whom they will develop a relationship. At the same time, it is vital for the Project Team to be structured appropriately with individuals being appointed leads in a variety of specialist knowledge areas such as civil engineering, planning, biodiversity management and people engagement.

In Steart, at this stage of consultation, it became important that local people and stakeholders in the landscape informed the Project Team about which values they placed on the landscape (Involve, 2005). The area's remoteness and distance from other people was recorded as a key value, as too was a 'ruralness' of the landscape and its management through agricultural practice. Recreational activities, such as walking and an inherent interest in the surrounding estuary, was strongly linked to a desire to be protected from flooding and future sea-level rise. Specifically, some of the fields or features within the area had a cultural and personal memorial value and the Project Team were determined to find ways these could be protected and accommodated within the design of the new embankment (Environment Agency/Bristol Port Company, 2011).

3.2.2 The local community's early perceptions towards the project

The creation of a landscape wetland with WWT's involvement brought out worries from local residents who valued the peninsula because of its sense of calm and naturalness. There was a deep concern that WWT's ambition would be to develop Steart Marshes into a major tourist destination, attracting hundreds of thousands of visitors a year. If true, these vastly polarised objectives would somehow need alignment to move forward positively. At an extremely early stage, WWT confirmed its position and made it clear that this was not its business objective, and it gave reassurances that through appropriate design and messaging, the visitor numbers would be controlled (Environment Agency and Bristol Port Company, 2011).

An evaluation of visitor numbers coming to the peninsula pre, during and post development was undertaken by specific visitor counts and surveys, which in turn was extrapolated against other similar sites around the UK's coastline (Planning Solutions Consulting Limited & DT Transport Planning, 2011). The results estimated that the annual pre-development level of around 10,000 visits would increase to around 40,000 once the site was constructed and the saltmarsh habitat had matured. Also, importantly, these figures were released to the community before planning permission was sought so there was time to discuss what this meant in practice and receive feedback. One key concern raised by local Steart residents was the increased likelihood of seeing visitors walking along the skyline of the new embankment. This resulted in positive dialogue about the location and shape of the new embankment and ultimately where the new footpath would be positioned. The final outcome of this was that the path was located predominantly at the base of the landward side of the sinuous bank with viewing access limited to just a few discreet areas, dispelling community fears, fulfilling community buy-in and offering a positive visitor experience.

Interestingly, recent visitor monitoring suggests that while this estimate is reasonably accurate there is still a sense of remoteness with few people around, and that is had been noted that local people walking to the site make up the majority of regular, daily visits. This has an indirect benefit of a positive sense of ownership as well as the practical gain of lower than expected movement of vehicles on the local roads. The latter was a particularly important consideration in terms of site design, and while the highway is a public asset, previous use had been predominantly from local residents. This had been identified as where the strongest feeling of disruption to local life would come from. In response to this, vehicle passing places were constructed along the single track approach road and the visitor car park was positioned at the southern end of the realignment site away from Steart village, reducing the overall distance that vehicles would be on the road (Halcrow, 2010a). Additionally, signage erected directing visitors to the car park helped reduce car use on non-direct roads.

3.3 Determining consultation styles

Aside from the vast experience of delivering civil engineering projects and habitat creation projects on a landscape scale, a significant part of the Project Team's capability was the friendliness and approachability of all the individuals appointed. It is impossible to put a team together based on this attribute alone but by default this happened, and it enabled two significant principles to occur:

- A culture of openness was embedded into every part of the project both internally and externally. This meant that the team was able to work as a cohesive unit, and trust rapidly built around the strengths, abilities and contribution each member brought to the project.
- A culture of transparency with an open-door policy was established so local residents could call into the site office and speak to a team member at a time that suited them. It was vital that the style of language used in conversation was neither overly technical nor too casual, and neither confrontational nor condescending.

Designed to be courteous, constructive and helpful in engaging conversation, face-to-face dialogue was used as a rule to resolve issues positively and amicably. A meeting area designed into the site office space meant that local residents could visit and talk in private about concerns they had. This space also housed presentation equipment enabling the project plans to be easily visualised. In addition, having a site office in the heart of the landscape also meant that invitations to individuals' homes within the community where concerns could be discussed in a relaxed and familiar environment could be easily accepted. Following any meeting, all actions were discussed among the Project Team, followed up and reported back, whether the outcome was positive or negative. This gave the community a strong sense that every issue was important and that they were being listened to. At times, when it was important to talk to larger community groups, village halls were used enabling local people easy access to a familiar venue.

This 'being available' approach coupled with the more formal and regular monthly public meetings gave an opportunity for both the Project Team to discuss the work plan for the month ahead and the local community to formally raise concerns. In 2020, some 11 years after the first public meeting and six years after the breach was created and the site became tidal, this forum still exists under the governance of the local parish councils that rotate chairmanship. Equally, the appointment of a dedicated local community liaison officer by the Environment Agency throughout the duration of the project helped coalesce the interests of the local communities and individuals on the Steart Peninsula and set up a mechanism that resulted in a bond of trust. The officer's ability to listen, empathise and calmly communicate the aims of the project was recorded as a positive experience by the local community (Wildfowl & Wetlands Trust, 2010). It is strongly advised that investing resources into engagement and communication from the onset of a project is not underestimated, as time and patience is critical in taking individuals on a journey of acceptance.

Alongside this, appointing WWT as the future site manager at a very early stage meant that the time invested in building open dialogue with local people paid dividends. This resulted in ensuring that WWT site staff were recognised as members of the local community and that WWT was a good organisation to work with and trust. This mutual benefit meant that a close partnership between the EA and WWT was formed. Together they created engagement techniques that aided an understanding of the predicted landscape change that would come from delivering the project. An example of this was through inviting local residents to visit and talk to other local coastal communities where coastal realignment had taken place, enabling open and honest conversation about the real and perceived changes ahead, seeing first-hand what those changes actually looked like.

Also, holding events that local residents had the first or only access to was important in terms of relationship building specifically. Immediately prior to the breach being excavated, local people were invited into the landscape for the last time before the tide eventually reclaimed the land. Evening walks along the bed of what would become the vast tidal creek were poignant and photographs of locals within this area have now become historical poignant. Prior to this, the archaeological excavation discovered significant finds with prehistoric, Romano-British and medieval discoveries reflecting the influence people have had on the landscape over thousands of years (Murphy et al., 2009). Excavation and demonstration enabled local residents to experience the lives of previous occupants of the peninsula; having direct access to this gave an important sense of discovery. Inviting the local primary school to experience this also added to the special nature of this forgotten landscape, which has lain hidden under the feet of local residents for centuries. Working with artists and storytellers, WWT was able to find imaginative ways to recreate scenes of what life within the landscape would have historically looked like.

3.4 Working with a skill base from the local community

Developing a positive and trusting relationship with local people was critically important for WWT, with long-term site managers having both moral and physical support from the community helped aid the delivery of on-going daily management. As trust between the local community and the Project Team grew, local people began to come forward to offer help to WWT as future site managers. The interest in becoming involved was incredibly positive and the project manager worked closely with ornithologists and botanists from the local villages who were prepared to give their time to help survey species.

This early interest has now led to the development of a 50-strong volunteer workforce, predominantly in the form of local people offering their time and skills to assist in a variety of voluntary roles including practical management activities, species monitoring and visitor engagement (Wildfowl & Wetlands Trust, 2019). Being able to define these roles and offer training and support in upskilling shows an important willingness in wanting to work with local people. A significant boost to this was WWT successfully being awarded a contract by the Environment Agency (EA) to undertake four years of biological monitoring work. To deliver this, the proposal included training local people in the necessary skills to complete surveys and monitoring. This resulted in a legacy which remains today with volunteers still completing monitoring work, aiding understanding of the biological changes that managed realignment brings. Six years since the site's creation, this team supports not only WWT in running Steart Marshes but critically helps inform visitors and other local residents about the value they experience while visiting the reserve.

The appointment of a permanent engagement officer role, a position filled by a member of the local community, further confirmed WWT's commitment to investing in local people. Through this engagement, whereby WWT communicates directly and indirectly with the local community, local people have effectively become ambassadors for the new landscape and the area's intrinsic appeal. More specifically, the positive value local people have placed on the site is now embedded within the heart of the local villages.

Since the reserve's completion, events such as open days, guided walks and creating trails, including willow sculptures by local artists and places to explore wetlands through pond dipping, have increased the appeal of the site to families (Wildfowl & Wetlands Trust, 2018). At the same time, these open activities are low key and coupled with wider advertising for events where people have to book, making the activity manageable in terms of numbers. An example of the latter are the popular Land Rover safaris where visitors have safe and guided access to areas that are usually unavailable, frequently led by skilled volunteer wardens from the local communities.

3.5 Providing additional societal benefits

The design of the site includes a network of new level-surface paths with gentle gradients, which provides improved access for both walkers and those with limited mobility. The viewing points and birdwatching hides, landscaped with natural timber and constructed in gentle curves, both reduce the impact on the skyline and the local landscape. Positioned on top of the new flood banks, they provide a destination point and give visitors a sense of anticipation as they reach the viewpoint where the vast, newly created landscape is revealed to them. This design was specifically undertaken to engage visitors with a sense of reaching a landscape of considerable scale, which constantly changes with tides and seasons (Halcrow, 2010b). Opportunities for adults with learning difficulties to be involved in site management activities has also led to regular visits from a local care provider.

These paths are also suitable for recreational activities such as horse riding and cycling with one route constructed to be 5 km in length, which is of particular interest to runners. These additional benefits mean the landscape now allows a wide range of people to access the area, something that was previously unavailable as the land had been under multiple private ownership. Demand to access the coast within the UK remains stable, though it is known that over 35% use the coast for heath and recreation purposes, which reflects the value people put on accessing wide-open horizons in remote coastal locations (TNS, 2016). It has also been recognised at Steart that local people who visit the site do so for quiet recreation, which brings with it a place for mindfulness and increased well-being. This is facilitated by having the focus of access around the car park at the southern point of the new reserve, meaning the residents of Steart village still retain their sense of remoteness. The car park has capacity for about 50 vehicles, yet during busy times the reserve still feels uncrowded due to its wide-open horizons and array of paths that help disperse people around the reserve. This has in part led to local entrepreneurialism with local pubs advertising local food and drink as part of a circular 5 km walk (Halcrow, 2011a, 2011b).

Agriculture remains one of the biggest management tools that will continue to shape and enhance the biodiversity value of the newly developing landscape (Halcrow, 2009). In general, allowing the tide to reclaim land that was itself reclaimed through engineering techniques hundreds of years ago, is often challenging for the agricultural community to accept. Having invested time and resources to farm the landscape for generations, naturally there was resistance to it being reclaimed by the tide. However, working with local famers WWT identified opportunities to continue managing the whole landscape productively, producing an agricultural income that pays for the running of the new nature reserve and delivers national biodiversity objectives (Mossman, 2012). Extensive cow and sheep grazing takes place across the site, with local farmers investing in traditional breed stock that thrives on less agriculturally productive land. In other areas, cropping produces wheat but with margins that grow native seed-bearing plants for wintering farmland birds to feed on. In addition, across the newly developing intertidal habitat cattle and sheep extensively graze; they are then sold at market at premium values as 'saltmarsh meat', which has a specialised, niche market (da Silva, 2012). This process of demonstration shows that managed realignment is still achievable and profitable within modern agriculture and again provides an income into the local economy, helping to emphasise a willingness to support the local community (Sedgemoor District Council, 2003).

Six years and over 600 tidal inundations later, the saltmarsh habitat at Steart Marshes has rapidly developed across a vast wetland landscape, and with it has come extensive research and measurement of its benefits from carbon sequestration to local economic investment (Pontee et al., 2015). As the site has matured and the extensive network of paths explored, the emphasis on promoting this site as a working wetland, a site of demonstration and good practice, continues to remain strong. The driver to create such sites comes predominantly from UK government contributions, creating international habitat that is being lost through anthropogenic means (Halcrow, 2010c). However, while this remains true, a focus towards a clearer understanding of what managed realignment contributes to carbon net zero targets is currently being undertaken and could potentially aid greater acceptability of such projects. Regardless of this outcome, from a local stakeholder perspective this landscape change will remain an important part of why the area they chose to live in is important and special. Now, every winter the Steart Peninsula is home to over 28,000 waterfowl that visit from northern and eastern Europe and is becoming increasingly important for the number of notably scarce breeding wading birds, such as little ringed plover, avocet and in 2020, black-winged stilt.

3.6 An exemplar of engagement and design

Not one landscape habitat creation scheme could ever be the same as another, but the principles behind working with stakeholders should be adhered to in order to achieve a positive outcome. The work to create Steart Marshes was delivered through an air of openness and honesty, and most challenges and protestation arose either through genuine misunderstanding or in rare cases because it suited another agenda. The latter was particularly noted during times of political electioneering and an attempt to draw Steart Marshes into wider, unrelated discussions on riparian flood defence management elsewhere on the Somerset Levels. However public reaction to unsubstantiated comments showed overall support for the creation of Steart Marshes (Bridgwater Mercury, 2014). While such large projects can inevitably get caught up in local politics, it is essential to remain focused on the benefits that they would bring to the local community (BBC, 2014). Also, at completion of the project it is critical to say 'thank you' and show appreciation to those from the local community who have been involved throughout. At Steart Marshes this was achieved by having a celebration event where local people and the Project Team had an afternoon BBQ in Steart village. This culminated in a walk to the new embankment to watch the first ever tide flowing through the newly constructed breach.

Today WWT are the proud land managers of Steart Marshes and regularly celebrates its successes with the local community. Volunteer numbers continue to increase and with over 50 people, our expectations have been exceeded. It remains an exemplar of landscape-scale habitat design and creation and alongside its programme of continued community engagement, is held in high acclaim as a blueprint in working with local people to achieve rapid landscape change. However, such an achievement not only requires time and resources but also involves the right people with the right skills to develop lasting, trusted relationships. The Project Team of engineers, designers, ecologists and project managers had all of those skills in plentiful supply, and by working closely as a team, the communication between individuals was exemplary. Equally, being available to listen to local people reinforced that feeling of worth and value; following up with a response and action made the whole liaison process effective and long lasting.

3.7 Implication for future practice and research needs

3.7.1 Implication for future practice

- Do not underestimate the time required to invest in communication.
- Early contractor and site manager involvement significantly helps efficiencies in the final design of the scheme, especially with knowledge of civil engineering, biodiversity management and people engagement techniques.

- Listen to and act on the concerns of the local community and understand the multiple values they place on their local landscape.
- Follow through with discussions and report back, whether positive or negative.
- Ensure a meeting area is designed into the site office that is both appropriate in scale and sufficiently large for internal and external meetings. This facilitates a focus for site-specific communication.
- Find long lasting ways of getting the community involved in the decision-making process: hold workshops on the position of public paths and viewing points; suggest the local community offer possible names for the site; and of course allow them to make suggestions on landscape planning and follow through on delivering enhancements etc.
- Identify ways (with the future site manager) to involve and engage with the existing skills, knowledge and interests of the local community.
- Partnerships bring in external funding from grant givers who may otherwise be unavailable to give to a single organisation.
- Invest time and financial resource in providing a community engagement officer who is trusted and respected by the local community. Bring alongside them a representative of the future site management body at a very early stage to ensure continuation of trust once the project has been completed and the CEO withdraws.

3.7.2 Future research needs

- To further the evidence around the multiple benefits of wetlands
- To research the contribution that coastal realignment makes to blue carbon
- To identify the water quality benefits of newly created saltmarshes
- To identify the biodiversity relationship that Steart Marshes has with its wider wetland landscape
- To advance our knowledge around the contribution coastal wetlands have to people's health and well-being
- To create detailed accounts on the economic impact that coastal realignment brings

References

Adam, P. (2002) Salt marshes in a time of change. *Environmental Conservation*, 29, 39–61.

Allen, J. et al. (1998) Medium-term sedimentation on high intertidal mudflats and salt marshes in the Severn Estuary, SW Britain: The role of wind and tide. *Marine Geology*, 150, 1–7.

Atkins (2013) *Severn Estuary Flood and Coastal Risk Management Strategy*. Devon: Environment Agency.

BBC (2014) online https://www.bbc.co.uk/news/uk-england-somerset-26952881

Black & Veatch (2009) Preferred Parrett Estuary Flood Risk Management Strategy Report Appendix E Geomorphology. Environment Agency.

Bridgwater Mercury (2014) online https://www.bridgwatermercury.co.uk/news/11463948.completed-steart-marshes-project-slammed-by-bridgwater-mp/

da Silva, L. (2012) *Ecosystem Services Assessment at Steart Peninsula*. Somerset, UK.

Defra/Environment Agency (2010) Understanding the Processes for Community Adaptation Planning and Engagement (CAPE) on the Coast. R&D Technical Report, FD2624/TR.

Environment Agency (2007) Working with others: Building trust with communities – A Guide for Staff.

Environment Agency (2010) Steart Coastal Management Project Community Consultation Exhibition Boards.

Environment Agency/Bristol Port Company (2011) Steart Coastal Management Project Master Plan for the Steart Peninsula. Environment Agency.

Halcrow (2009) Steart Coastal Management Project, Phase One Review. Environment Agency.

Halcrow (2010a) Steart Coastal Management Project Scoping Consultation Document Summary Report. Environment Agency.

Halcrow (2010b) Steart Coastal Management Project Environmental Statement. Environment Agency.

Halcrow (2010c) Steart Coastal Management Project, Ecological Review. Environment Agency.

Halcrow (2011a) Steart Coastal Management Project Statement of Community Consultation. Environment Agency.

Halcrow (2011b) Steart Coastal Management Project Summary of Environmental Impacts. Environment Agency.

Humber Community Project (2008) Lessons learned and best practice in community engagement on changing coasts. *Coastal Futures.* Humber: Humber Community Project.

Involve (2005) *People & Participation: How to put citizens at the heart of decision-making*. London: Involve.

Mossman, H. (2012) Does managed coastal realignment create saltmarshes with 'equivalent biological characteristics' to natural reference sites? Journal of Applied Ecology, 49(6), 1446–1456.

Murphy P. et al. (2009) Coastal heritage and climate change in England: assessing threats and priorities. *Conservation and Management of Archeological Sites*, 11(1), 9–15.

Pethick, J. S. (2002) Managed realignment within Bridgwater Bay and the River Parrett. Preliminary geomorphological assessment. 22pp. Environment Agency.

Planning Solutions Consulting Limited & DT Transport Planning (2011) Steart Coastal Management Project Visitor Assessment Final Report. Environment Agency.

Pontee, N. et al. (2015) Delivering Large Habitat Restoration Schemes: Lessons from the Steart Coastal Management Project.

Sedgemoor District Council (2003) Sedgemoor Landscape Assessment and Countryside Design Summary.

TNS (2016) *Monitor of Engagement with the Natural Environment.* Natural England.

Wildfowl & Wetlands Trust (2010) Steart Pathfinder Project Community Engagement – formal learning activities with Otterhampton School. Environment Agency.

Wildfowl & Wetlands Trust (2018) Steart Marshes Willow Sculpture Trail downloadable from https://www.wwt.org.uk/blog/wp-content/uploads/2016/08/WWT-Steart-Marshes-Willow-Sculptures.pdf

Wildfowl & Wetlands Trust (2019) A dedicated volunteer. Accessed via https://www.wwt.org.uk/wetland-centres/steart-marshes/news/2019/04/03/dick-a-dedicated-volunteer/16653

Wessex Archaeology (2010) Steart Coastal Management Project Heritage Assessment. Environment Agency.

4 People's perceptions towards the Steart Marshes Creation Project through stakeholder interviews and questionnaires

Robert J. McInnes, Mark Everard and Hiromi Yamashita

4.1 Introduction and method summary

4.1.1 The restoration project summary

The Steart Coastal Management Project in Somerset is one of the largest managed realignment projects to have been delivered in the UK (Scott et al., 2016). As with other similar initiatives elsewhere in the UK and beyond, a range of stakeholders are interested in the perceptions and attitudes of local communities with regards to 'softer' approaches to coastal management (Myatt-Bell et al., 2002; Goeldner-Gianella, 2007). The realignment of flood defences and the restoration of some 400 ha of coastal wetlands at the Steart Peninsula provided the opportunity to investigate what people living adjacent to Europe's largest coastal restoration schemes think about the project, and to evaluate their responses. Their insight might resonate beyond the shores of the Severn Estuary.

4.1.2 Research methods

Two principal methods were utilised to assess public perception of the restoration of Steart Marshes. First, individual and group semi-structured interviews were conducted; and second, a questionnaire was distributed by post and electronically across the local community. The questionnaire was sent to all 417 households in the constituencies of the Steart Coastal Management Project. The questionnaire was posted together with the local newsletter, which contained an article explaining the research project and questionnaire. The response rate was 24.2%,

DOI: 10.4324/9780367863098-4

with 101 questionnaires returned. Of the respondents, 81.8% were over 50 years old, including more than 61.6% over 60 years old. More than 90% of the respondents had been living in area for over 10 years.

Field visits to the Steart Peninsula were conducted in September 2013, and in February and September 2014. In total, 27 in-depth interviews were held, including four people who were interviewed before and after the restoration activities had taken place. All the interviews were from the local community in and around the Steart Peninsula and included inter alia local residents, landowners, local government officials and members and representatives of environmental groups.

Through these research activities, we hoped to:

- identify various evaluation indicators of risks and benefits of a restoration project set by different stakeholders; and
- analyse commonalities and differences of discourses, and of stories of risks and benefits of restoration between different stakeholders.

It is well established that lay people accrue and apply knowledge about their local environment, especially with regards to flood risk, in multiple ways (McEwen and Jones, 2012). Understanding local reasoning was considered critical for evaluating the perceptions of risks and benefits. As has been demonstrated elsewhere (Landström et al., 2011), local knowledge, though not construed as 'scientific' in a classical sense, can provide valuable insight into mapping and understanding flood risk. Consequently, the hypothesis that differences in opinion arise simply due to a 'lack of knowledge' was roundly rejected as an over-simplistic assumption. The objective of the study was to unpick subtleties in perception through the interview methods and questionnaires to understand the reasons behind the views that people hold. In addition, the study aimed to identify the principles used by citizens when discussing the risks and benefits of the Steart Coastal Management Project.

All interviews were transcribed and coded with computer assisted qualitative data analysis MaxQDA software (https://www.maxqda.com). Analysis was conducted using thematic coding, which identified transcribed text linked by a common theme or idea allowing the researchers to index the text into categories and establish a framework of thematic ideas about it (Gibbs, 2007).

4.2 Findings from the individual and group interviews

The principal comments from interviewees regarding the risks and benefits of the Steart Coastal Management Project are summarised in

Table 4.1 Summary of the risks and benefits of the project expressed by the interviewees for the Steart case

Benefits	A "new stronger sea defence", which divides the village and the re-flooded area "New footpaths" and "new horse-riding routes", which link nearby villages A "resting place for birds" "A good opportunity for the farmers to sell their lands", which could be "under the water" in the future
Risks	"Too many visitors coming to the quiet local area" "Possible road accident" "Limited access to the area" during the high tide "Loss of fertile farmlands" "No views with cows" "Salinity in ditches [for farmland]"

Table 4.1. Many of these elements were identified in the comprehensive programme of consultation conducted by the Environment Agency (EA), the government environmental regulator in England, during the development of the project (EA, 2011).

Codification of the information captured in the interviews allows a visualisation of the relationships among the observations. The individual risks and benefits have been plotted along two axes: geographical proximity (personal–local–national/global) and probability of those risks and benefits occurring (certain–less certain–uncertain). Linkages among and between the risks and benefits are indicated by arrows.

Two main observations emerge from this visualisation. First, citizens characteristically made links between personal/certain risks and benefits and wider/uncertain risks and benefits. Previous research on social perceptions towards coastal realignment projects commonly conclude that citizens only or mainly respond to tangible project benefits, such as access to footpaths, and are more sceptical about flood risk benefits (Esteves and Thomas, 2014) . By contrast, citizens spoke about both tangible and personal risks and benefits arising from the managed realignment project, together with local/national/global risks and benefits.

Second, significant gaps were observed between the views of local citizens and 'environmentalists'. Within the interviews, three subjects were not highlighted by local citizens, but were key considerations for the government body responsible for the management and maintenance of flood defences in England and the organisation responsible for the long-term management of the site. These three views (dashed ellipses

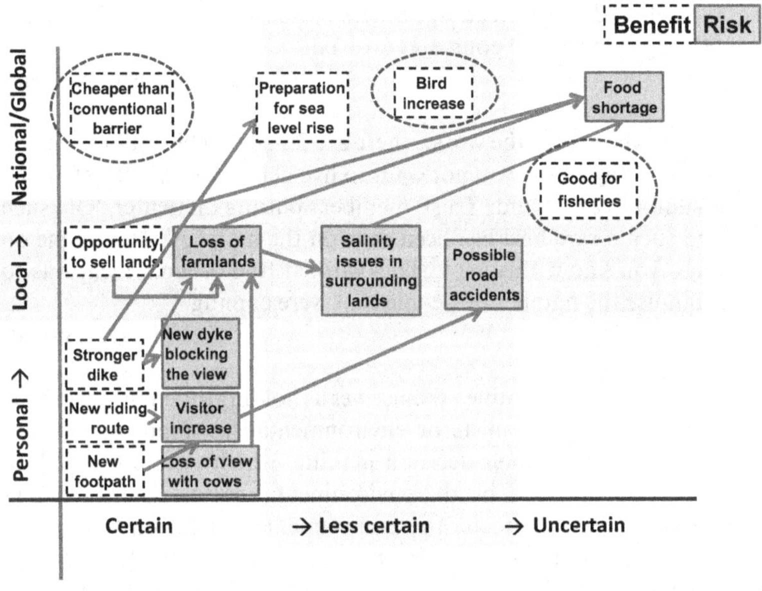

Figure 4.1 Personal/global and certain/uncertain risk benefit grid for stated benefits and risks in the interviews.

in Figure 4.1) were that the project would be cheaper than constructing a conventional flood defence barrier (certain national/global benefit); bird numbers would increase (less certain national/global benefit); and the scheme would be good for local fisheries (less certain national/global benefit).

The EA is responsible for the strategic overview of coastal flood management in England. Increasingly, part of the role of the EA is to engage with local communities to identify how they can benefit from managed realignment projects, such as the proposals for the Steart Peninsula (Thomas, 2014). It was highlighted in the interviews that the local EA staff had been highly engaged in the project and proactively sought to work with the local community in realising their desired outcomes. Consequently, the realignment project developed a friendly relationship between the residents and the contractors working on behalf of the EA. However, some interviewees clearly differentiated the approach of the EA and that of other environmental organisations. For example:

> The Somerset Levels, there's tons of wildlife out there. It's always been there. All they're doing is replacing one type of wildlife with

> another and they'll say, 'Oh, you know, so we have to suppress one type of wildlife to encourage others'. Well, I'd rather let our wildlife take its own natural course. It evolved.
>
> (Stockland Bristol resident)

> It's like the end of the world; there are 20-30,000 birds down here in winter. Why would you not want to live here? … [but] We get WWT [Wildfowl & Wetlands Trust] members putting on twitter, 'Oh, such and such a rare bird has been seen on the marshes'. Hey, come on guys, you know, this is our backyard. It [the original idea] was to minimise the number of people that were coming.
>
> (Steart resident)

Several interviewees identified themselves as holding different viewpoints from nature conservationists or environmentalists, applying different evaluation criteria in their decision making, which were not based on the discourses provided by the environmental sector. The interviews demonstrated that the greater the environmentalists' attempts to justify the restoration on nature conservation grounds, the less local people became engaged and interested in the project. This perspective resulted from a divergence in the perception of the benefits.

The role of a neutral body to mediate the process of delivering a managed realignment project to develop a consensus and move towards implementation has been recognised elsewhere in the UK (Midgley and McGlashan, 2004). Although some of the comments from local interviewees were simple statements of different views, neither negative nor positive, divergent viewpoints and perceptions expressed by the local residents and environmentalists could potentially develop into implementation barriers between these constituencies. This separation of 'us' (residents) and 'them' (environmentalists) had the potential to continue to hinder the success of this and other projects, as external visitors coming to the restored site for recreation, such as bird watching might be seen as new environmentalists, having an undesirable impact on the local community.

4.3 Findings from the questionnaire data

4.3.1 Mental images and functions

Out of all responses, more than half (51.5%) of the respondents reported thinking that the coastal environment in and around the Severn Estuary is "getting better", while only around 10% of them reported the environment is "not changing" or "getting worse". However, the proportion

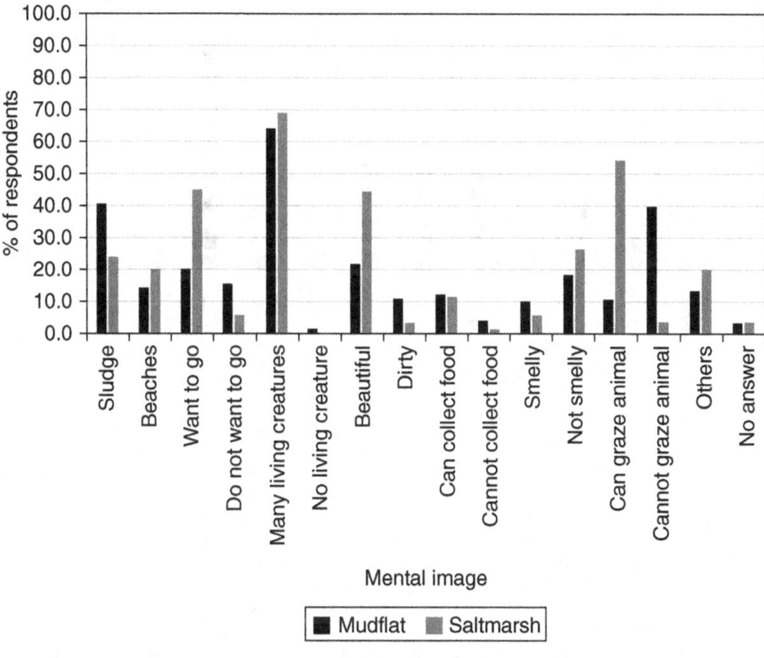

Figure 4.2 Mental image of saltmarshes and mudflats at Steart Marshes.

of respondents who replied "do not know" regarding changes in the coastal environment in and around the Seven Estuary was close to a quarter of respondents (21.8%).

The mental image of saltmarshes was predominantly positive, with 69.3% of the respondents choosing "many living creatures" and approximately 55% reporting "can graze animals" (Figure 4.2). Additionally, almost 45% of the respondents had a mental image of saltmarshes being "beautiful" and somewhere that they "want to go". However, 25% of the respondents viewed saltmarshes as "sludge". Compared to the mental image of saltmarshes, the commonly perceived image of mudflats among the respondents was more negative. Even though nearly 65% of the respondents chose mudflats have "many living creatures", the choices of "sludge" (40.6%) and "cannot graze animals" (39.6%) were the two most commonly selected images of mudflats. Similar to saltmarshes, the most common function of mudflats selected by the respondents was "provides areas for birds to rest and feed" (88.1%).

The dominant function of saltmarshes and mudflats identified by the respondents was they "provide areas for birds to rest or feed" (90.1%

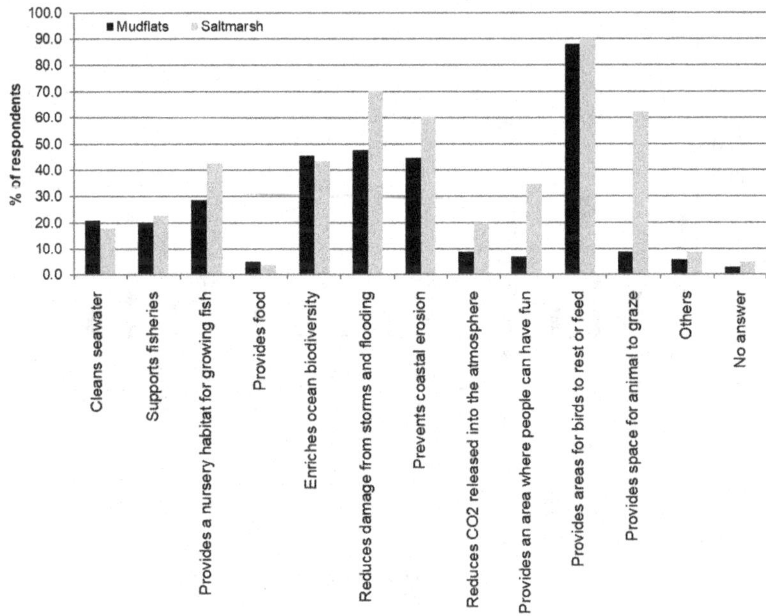

Figure 4.3 Perception of the functions of saltmarshes and mudflats at Steart Marshes.

and 88.1% respectively) (Figure 4.3). Respondents also recognised the following functions as being present relatively frequently at saltmarshes: "reduces damage from storms and flooding" (70.3%); "provides space for animals to graze" (62.4%); and "prevents coastal erosion" (60.4%). Less than 20% of the respondents agreed that saltmarshes can help to "clean seawater" (17.8%) and "reduce CO_2 released into the atmosphere" (19.8%); and only 4% reported they "provide food". For mudflats, three functions were reported to be of relatively high importance, namely "reduces damage from storms and flooding" (47.5%); "enriches ocean biodiversity" (45.5%); and "prevents coastal erosion" (44.6%). The role of mudflats in preventing erosion and flooding was considered less than for saltmarshes. A significant difference, unsurprisingly, was the fact that mudflats are considered less likely to "provide space for animals to graze" (8.9%).

About 80% of questionnaire respondents felt positive about the Steart Marshes project, and 52.5% of them reported feeling "very positive". However, in statements about the relationship between the project and farmland, the respondents seemed ambivalent. Many of them chose "neutral" for questions such as, "the project represents a loss of productive farmland"; "the project is desirable since it returns farmland to the sea, which was the original state"; and "the project enhances the coastal environment, which is more important than keeping farmland".

Respondents were asked to describe how they would consider the Steart Marshes project to be a success. As this was an open, free text response, numerous elements and indicators were mentioned. The most popular categories of success indicators (with the number of times respondents used these or similar terms in parenthesis) were as follows in order: enhancing biodiversity and wildlife, including birds (42); being an attractive space for recreation and exercise (31); reducing the risk of flooding (15); providing a place for learning and education (12); and being a local attraction (7). Only six respondents indicated that they perceived the project to be unsuccessful.

4.3.2 Understanding ecosystem services

In the questionnaire, the 11 functions explicitly mentioned are synonymous with ecosystem services provided by coastal wetlands. However, the functions presented in the questionnaire do not represent an expansive or definitive list of the full range of ecosystem services likely to be delivered at Steart Marshes. A qualitative assessment indicated that the site provided 29 ecosystem services (da Silva et al., 2014), whereas the questionnaire targeted 11 functions. This approach potentially brings a bias to the reporting, but similar challenges exist in the application of other non-systemic assessment techniques, which only consider a subset of ecosystem services, commonly applied in the evaluation of ecosystem services delivered by managed realignment projects. For instance, an assessment of five ecosystem services was conducted on Hesketh Outmarch West and the Inner Firth of Forth, both in the UK, using the TESSA (Toolkit for Ecosystem Services Site-based Assessment) approach (MacDonald et al., 2017), while an economic valuation study on the restoration of a tidal marsh system in the Schelde Estuary targeted 15 ecosystem services (Boerema et al., 2016).

The responses to the questionnaire represent a form of citizen science ('science by non-scientists') (Paul et al., 2018), which sought to understand perception rather than a traditional scientific assessment of all or individual ecosystem services. Nevertheless, the perceptions of the different functions shed light on the local understanding of the benefits that managed realignment projects can deliver and how these are perceived. There is good evidence from the scientific literature that

Table 4.2 Evidence of ecosystem service delivery associated with managed realignment projects

Ecosystem service category	*Ecosystem service ('function')*	*Evidence*
Provisioning	Provides space for animal to graze	Ford et al. (2012) Davidson et al. (2017)
	Provides food	da Silva et al. (2014) MacDonald et al. (2017)
Regulating	Cleans seawater	Andrews et al. (2006) Chang et al. (2001)
	Reduces damage from storms and flooding	Ledoux et al. (2005) MacDonald et al. (2017)
	Prevents coastal erosion	Symonds and Collins (2007) Williams et al. (2018)
	Reduces CO_2 released into the atmosphere	Andrews et al. (2006) Beaumont et al. (2014) da Silva et al. (2014) MacDonald et al. (2017)
Cultural	Provides an area where people can have fun	da Silva et al. (2014) MacDonald et al. (2017)
Supporting	Provides areas for birds to rest or feed	Atkinson et al. (2004) Mander et al. (2007)
	Supports fisheries	Colclough et al. (2005) MacDonald et al. (2017)
	Provides a nursery habitat for growing fish	Colclough et al. (2005) Fonseca (2009)
	Enriches ocean biodiversity	Eertman et al. (2002) Nunn et al. (2012)

managed realignment of similar coastal systems in the UK, and elsewhere in north west Europe, deliver on all 11 functions assessed in the questionnaire (Table 4.2). However, their relative importance will depend on overcoming barriers to accessing benefits (Wieland et al., 2016) and their relative value in both monetary and non-monetary or intangible terms (Klain and Chan, 2012).

The respondents seemed very much aware of at least some of the regulating and supporting services of saltmarshes and mudflats (even if not expressing it in those technical terms). However, several regulating services, particularly cleaning seawater and the role of coastal habitats in mitigating CO_2 release, were not well recognised. Similarly, the role of both the habitats in providing food (such as shellfish, samphire, fish or productive grazing land) was poorly recognised. Therefore, there are clear gaps in public perception of certain functions that deviate from the scientific knowledge base. However, the failure to recognise wetland ecosystem services may be more endemic and not just a challenge for local citizens. In an analysis of the ecosystem services provided by four Ramsar sites in southern England, including three coastal wetlands, McInnes (2013) demonstrates that the gap between recognised and unrecognised ecosystem services has implications for the consideration of wetlands in decision making and the protection and wise use of all wetlands within Sussex and beyond.

Public perception at other managed realignment sites has demonstrated a concern over the loss of agricultural land, and hence a reduction in food production (Myatt et al., 2003). This too was raised as a concern for the areas where mudflats would dominate at Steart Marshes. It has also been demonstrated that public understanding of climate change adaptation of managed realignment is weak at other sites (Schliephack and Dickinson, 2017), and interpretation by lay people of the processes underpinning climate change, such as CO_2 dynamics in coastal wetlands, can be confused and poorly understood (Lorenzoni et al., 2007).

Potentially there is a disconnect between environmental organisations (governmental and non-governmental) and their messaging around cheaper costs and the benefits for fisheries and birds (the three priorities identified in Figure 4.4), and the knowledge gaps identified through the questionnaire responses, especially relating to food production, water quality improvements and climate change mitigation. Potentially, this exposes an area where environmental organisations may need to improve their messaging and communicate the public more effectively.

4.4 Project success indicators defined by citizens

Through the questionnaire, citizens were asked how much they agree or disagree with the restoration project in relation to a set of particular outcomes (Figure 4.4). The respondents showed a pattern of agreeing with positive statements about the Steart Marshes project and disagreeing with negative statements. A total of 66% of the respondents agreed or strongly agreed that the project "reduces the effects of natural disasters". Approximately 50% of the respondents agreed or strongly agreed that the managed realignment "creates a space where we can play or learn", "boosts the image of Steart Peninsula or Sedgemoor District", "compensates for the damage caused by other coastal development" and "has been implemented through a fair consultation process".

The main issues the respondents disagreed or strongly disagreed with were that the project "deprives the local residents of a quiet living

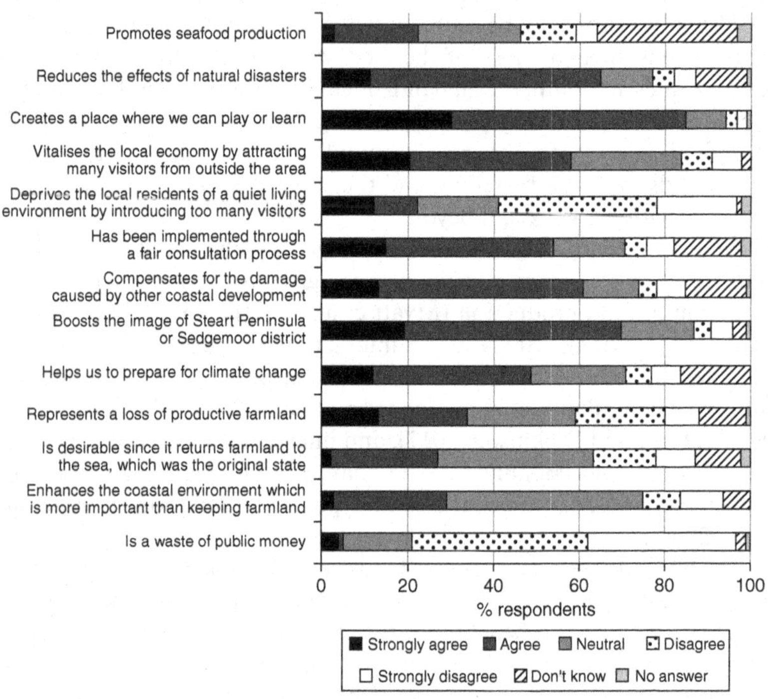

Figure 4.4 Degree of public agreement in overall project outcomes.

environment by introducing too many visitors" and "the project is a waste of public money". This suggests that the local respondents felt that the project represents good value for money and does not have a significant impact on the local residents through increased public access. Possibly, the management role of an organisation such as WWT, with decades of experience in managing sensitive sites for people and wildlife (Spray, 2018) combined with their inclusive consultative approach to site design, which has been demonstrated to reduce potential conflicts elsewhere (Reynolds and Elson, 1996), has assisted in mitigating the impact of visitors on the local community. However, in terms of the statements about the relationship between the project and farmland, the respondents seemed ambivalent. Many of them chose 'neutral' for questions such as "the project represents a loss of productive farmland" or "the project is desirable since it returns farmland to the sea, which was the original state".

4.5 Conclusion: Implications for future practice and research needs

This chapter has explored the insights provided by the interview and questionnaire research from the Steart Coastal Management Project in Somerset, UK. The interview sampling strategy was opportunistic on and near the site and also included snowball sampling (non-probabilistic sampling) with the researchers attempting to contact as many of the local residents as possible, as well as people with various occupations and backgrounds. The distribution of the questionnaire was inclusive and reached out to all the immediate and wider households around the site. Therefore, there is relative high confidence in the findings of the study and the perceptions of the local community with regards to the risks and benefits of the project.

4.5.1 Implications for future practice

Based on the findings, the following key messages emerge from the research:

- Different risks and benefits are emphasised from the two different study approaches (interviews and questionnaire). This suggests that utilising both approaches can expose nuances in the perceptions of risks and benefits.
- The interviews highlighted support for the strengthened sea defences, the new access paths, a resting place for birds and a good opportunity for farmers to sell their land. The questionnaires emphasised the reduced impact of natural disasters, the benefits of developing a place to play and learn, the image of the local area and the importance of good engagement and consultation.
- Analysis of the interviews demonstrates that citizens understand the tangible and personal benefits as well as more nebulous and uncertain national or global issues. The analysis also suggests that local citizens' desired benefits differ from those of environmental organisations such as the EA or WWT. This has important implications for messaging and awareness raising from and by environmental organisations.
- Responses provided during the interview process also emphasise the importance of a genuinely participatory consultation process.
- The mental image of saltmarshes and mudflats were generally similar; however, subtle differences emerge from the analysis of the

questionnaire responses, with mudflats possessing a more negative image.

- Overall, the respondents felt positive about the outcomes of the managed realignment project, with enhanced biodiversity highlighted as the main indicator of success.

4.5.2 Future research needs

- A knowledge gap remains in the citizens' understanding of the functions or ecosystem services provided by saltmarshes and mudflats. Providing awareness raising and environmental education around the key knowledge gaps, such as understanding the role of coastal wetlands in climate change mitigation and the provision of food, should be considered in the future for other managed realignment schemes.

References

Andrews, J.E., Burgess, D., Cave, R.R., Coombes, E.G., Jickells, T.D., Parkes, D.J. and Turner, R.K. (2006) 'Biogeochemical value of managed realignment, Humber estuary, UK.' *Science of the Total Environment*, 371(1–3), 19–30.

Atkinson, P.W., Crooks, S., Drewitt, A., Grant, A., Rehfisch, M.M., Sharpe, J. and Tyas, C.J. (2004) 'Managed realignment in the UK – the first 5 years of colonization by birds.' *Ibis*, 146, 101–110.

Beaumont, N.J., Jones, L., Garbutt, A., Hansom, J.D. and Toberman, M. (2014) 'The value of carbon sequestration and storage in coastal habitats.' *Estuarine, Coastal and Shelf Science*, 137, 32–40.

Boerema, A., Geerts, L., Oosterlee, L., Temmerman, S. and Meire, P. (2016) 'Ecosystem service delivery in restoration projects: The effect of ecological succession on the benefits of tidal marsh restoration.' *Ecology and Society*, 21(2), 10.

Chang, Y.H., Scrimshaw, M.D., MacLeod, C.L. and Lester, J.N. (2001) 'Flood defence in the Blackwater Estuary, Essex, UK: The impact of sedimentological and geochemical changes on salt marsh development in the Tollesbury managed realignment site.' *Marine Pollution Bulletin*, 42(6), 469–480.

Colclough, S., Fonseca, L., Astley, T., Thomas, K. and Watts, W. (2005) 'Fish utilisation of managed realignments.' *Fisheries Management and Ecology*, 12(6), 351–360.

da Silva, L.V., Everard, M. and Shore, R.G. (2014) 'Ecosystem services assessment at Steart Peninsula, Somerset, UK.' *Ecosystem Services*, 10, 19–34.

Davidson, K.E., Fowler, M.S., Skov, M.W., Doerr, S.H., Beaumont, N. and Griffin, J.N. (2017) 'Livestock grazing alters multiple ecosystem properties and services in salt marshes: A meta-analysis.' *Journal of Applied Ecology*, 54(5), 1395–1405.

Eertman, R.H., Kornman, B.A., Stikvoort, E. and Verbeek, H. (2002) 'Restoration of the Sieperda tidal marsh in the Scheldt estuary, the Netherlands.' *Restoration Ecology*, 10(3), 438–449.

Environment Agency (2011) *Steart Coastal Management Project: Environmental Statement – Non-Technical Summary*. Bristol, UK: Environment Agency, p. 11.

Esteves, L.S. and Thomas, K. (2014) 'Managed realignment in practice in the UK: Results from two independent surveys.' *Journal of Coastal Research*, (70), 407–413.

Fonseca, L. (2009) *Fish utilisation of managed realignment areas and saltmarshes in the Blackwater Estuary, Essex, S.E. England*. PhD thesis. London: Queen Mary University of London.

Ford, H., Garbutt, A., Jones, D.L. and Jones, L. (2012) 'Impacts of grazing abandonment on ecosystem service provision: Coastal grassland as a model system.' *Agriculture, Ecosystems & Environment*, 16, 108–115.

Gibbs, G.R. (2007) 'Thematic coding and categorizing.' *Analyzing Qualitative Data*, 703, 38–56.

Goeldner-Gianella, L. (2007) 'Perceptions and attitudes toward de-polderisation in Europe: A comparison of five opinion surveys in France and the UK.' *Journal of Coastal Research*, 23(5 (235)), 1218–1230.

Klain, S.C. and Chan, K.M. (2012) 'Navigating coastal values: Participatory mapping of ecosystem services for spatial planning.' *Ecological Economics*, 82, 104–113.

Landström, C., Whatmore, S.J., Lane, S.N., Odoni, N.A., Ward, N. and Bradley, S. (2011) 'Coproducing flood risk knowledge: Redistributing expertise in critical "participatory modelling"'. *Environment and Planning A*, 43(7), 1617–1633.

Ledoux, L., Cornell, S., O'Riordan, T., Harvey, R. and Banyard, L. (2005) 'Towards sustainable flood and coastal management: Identifying drivers of, and obstacles to, managed realignment.' *Land Use Policy*, 22(2), 129–144.

Lorenzoni, I., Nicholson-Cole, S. and Whitmarsh, L. (2007) 'Barriers perceived to engaging with climate change among the UK public and their policy implications.' *Global Environmental Change*, 17(3-4), 445–459.

MacDonald, M.A., de Ruyck, C., Field, R.H., Bedford, A. and Bradbury, R. B. (2017) 'Benefits of coastal managed realignment for society: Evidence from ecosystem service assessments in two UK regions.' *Estuarine, Coastal and Shelf Science*, 105609.

Mander, L., Cutts, N.D., Allen, J. and Mazik, K. (2007) 'Assessing the development of newly created habitat for wintering estuarine birds.' *Estuarine, Coastal and Shelf Science*, 75(1-2), 163–174.

McEwen, L. and Jones, O. (2012) 'Building local/lay flood knowledges into community flood resilience planning after the July 2007 floods, Gloucestershire, UK.' *Hydrology Research*, 43(5), 675–688.

McInnes, R.J. (2013) 'Recognizing ecosystem services from wetlands of international importance: An example from Sussex, UK.' *Wetlands*, 33(6), 1001–1017.

Midgley, S. and McGlashan, D.J. (2004) 'Planning and management of a proposed managed realignment project: Bothkennar, Forth Estuary, Scotland.' *Marine Policy*, 28(5), 429–435.

Myatt, L.B., Scrimshaw, M.D. and Lester, J.N. (2003) 'Public perceptions and attitudes towards a current managed realignment scheme: Brancaster West Marsh, North Norfolk, UK.' *Journal of Coastal Research*, 19(2), 278–286.

Myatt-Bell, L.B., Scrimshaw, M.D., Lester, J.N. and Potts, J.S. (2002) 'Public perception of managed realignment: Brancaster west Marsh, North Norfolk, UK.' *Marine Policy*, 26(1), 45–57.

Nunn, A.D., Tewson, L.H. and Cowx, I.G. (2012) 'The foraging ecology of larval and juvenile fishes.' *Reviews in Fish Biology and Fisheries*, 22(2), 377–408.

Paul, J.D., Buytaert, W., Allen, S., Ballesteros-Cánovas, J.A., Bhusal, J., Cieslik, K., ... and Dewulf, A. (2018) 'Citizen science for hydrological risk reduction and resilience building.' *Wiley Interdisciplinary Reviews: Water*, 5(1), e1262.

Reynolds, G. and Elson, M.J. (1996) 'The sustainable use of sensitive countryside sites for sport and active recreation.' *Journal of Environmental Planning and Management*, 39(4), 563–576.

Scott, J., Pontee, N., McGrath, T., Cox, R. and Philips, M. (2016) Delivering large habitat restoration schemes: Lessons from the Steart Coastal Management Project. In: Baptiste, A. (ed.), *Coastal management: Changing coast, changing climate, changing minds.* London, UK: ICE Publishing, pp. 663–674.

Schliephack, J. and Dickinson, J.E. (2017) 'Tourists' representations of coastal managed realignment as a climate change adaptation strategy.' *Tourism Management*, 59, 182–192.

Spray, M.C. (2018) 'Wildfowl and Wetlands Trust.' In: Finlayson, C.M., Everard, M., Irvine, K., McInnes, R.J., Middleton, B., Van Dam, A.A. and Davidson, N.C. (eds.) *The wetland book: Structure and function, management and methods I.* Dordrecht, Netherlands: Springer, pp.717–726.

Symonds, A.M. and Collins, M.B. (2007) 'The development of artificially created breaches in an embankment as part of a managed realignment, Freiston Shore, UK.' *Journal of Coastal Research*, 130–134.

Thomas, K. (2014) 'Managed realignment in the UK: The role of the Environment Agency.' In: Esteves, L.S. (ed.) *Managed realignment: A viable long-term coastal management strategy?* Dordrecht, Netherlands: Springer, pp. 83–94.

Wieland, R., Ravensbergen, S., Gregr, E.J., Satterfield, T. and Chan, K.M. (2016) 'Debunking trickle-down ecosystem services: The fallacy of omnipotent, homogeneous beneficiaries.' *Ecological Economics*, 121, 175–180.

Williams, A.T., Rangel-Buitrago, N., Pranzini, E. and Anfuso, G. (2018) 'The management of coastal erosion.' *Ocean & Coastal Management*, 156, 4–20.

Case Study B information for Chapters 5 and 6

Kuala Gula Mangrove Rehabilitation Project, Kuala Gula, Perak District, Malaysia

Balu Perumal, Hiromi Yamashita, and Naoyuki Mikami

This grassroots project became nationally famous for providing community development and an income generating mechanism, alongside wetland restoration. The tight-knit community of fishers developed the project with national non-governmental organisations (NGOs), who placed personnel in the village for three years. However, the destruction of nearby mangrove forests for shrimp farming overshadowed the positive impact of the restoration project felt by the community. Despite many outside the Malay fisher community previously not knowing about their local restoration project, partly because of language barriers, strong support for it was found. Therefore, there is potential to strengthen the activities across various communities in the future.

Background of the Mangrove Rehabilitation Project in Kuala Gula

An accidental breach of the land reclaimed by drainage was the starting point of the Kuala Gula Mangrove Rehabilitation Project. With help from various bodies, the project started in 2003. Information regarding this site is as follows.

- During the English colonial era, this village was developed as sugar plantations. Kuala means 'where rivers meet', Gula means 'sugar'. The plantations were turned into coconuts and later palm oil plantations after the country's independence in 1957.
- Southeast Asia, including Malaysia, has been increasingly concerned about the loss of mangroves, which provide buffer zones for the surrounding environment as well as habitat for many living creatures.

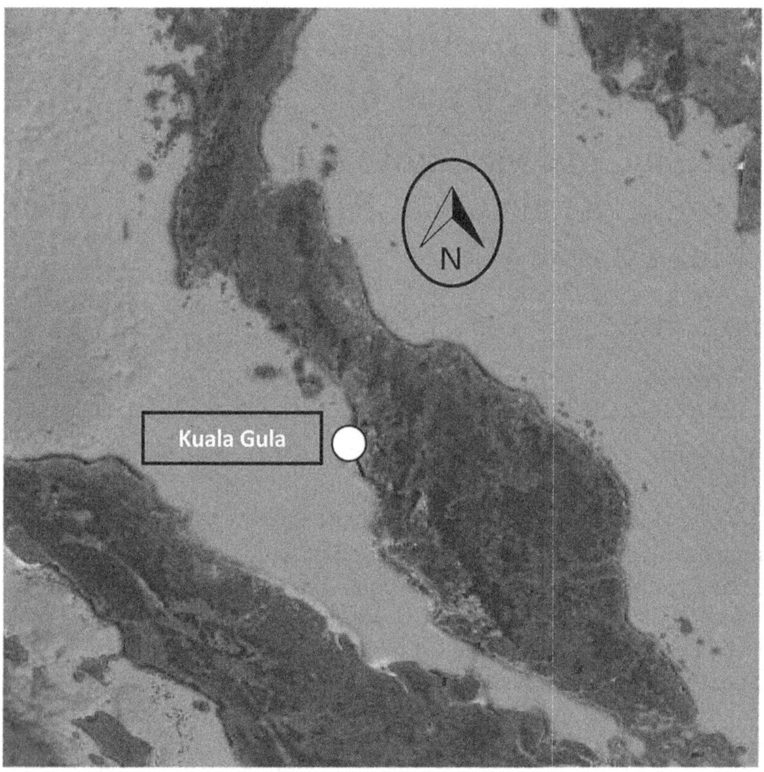

Figure B.1 Location of the Kuala Gula case study site.

- In 2004, tsunamis resulted from the earthquake in the Indian Ocean. In Thailand, a village was saved thanks to the mangrove in front of it absorbing the tsunami's energy. This incident inspired the governments in Southeast Asia to start investing in major mangrove plantation activities with government funding.
- In Malaysia, the 10th Malaysia Plan (2011–2015) and the 11th Malaysia Plan (2016–2020) set a target of planting 50 million mangrove trees. The Ministry of Natural Resources and Environment and the Prime Minister's Department have begun providing the budgets to meet these targets.
- In Kuala Gula, mangrove forests were cut down in the 1960s to create reclaimed land by drainage for village settlements known as Teluk Rubiah. The newly created land suffered from continuous flooding from the sea as the sea walls were naturally breached many

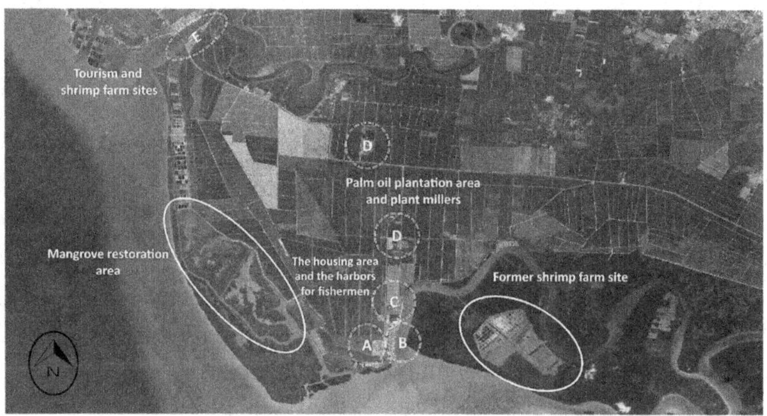

Figure B.2 Map of the project site and constituency.

Table B.1 Kuala Gula Mangrove Rehabilitation Project details

Site name	Kuala Gula Mangrove Rehabilitation Project
Location	Kuala Gula village, Perak, Malaysia
Project type	Mangrove Rehabilitation Project
Year implemented	In 2006, when the sea wall was naturally breached, the local fishers started to replant the mangroves, which had been cut down for village settlements. The mangrove restoration activities are ongoing
Size (ha)	608
Habitat(s) restored	Mangrove forests, tidal flats
Aims of the project	Rehabilitation of oceanic biodiversity, prevention of tsunami disasters, creation of environmental education site, creation of community managed forest site, turning planting activities into a tourist attraction
Project contractor	Environmental NGO (Global Environmental Centre, Malaysia)
Previous landowner	Local government
Stakeholders	Fishers, citizens, tourist operators, local and national governments, local and national NGOs
Number of communities within the constituency	6 (1 Malay, 3 Chinese, 2 plantations)
Population	6,371 people (estimated by the Kuala Kurau Sub-district office)

times and the government gave up repairing them. The population moved and now reside at the present Kuala Gula village. Over the last 10 years, new housing development projects have grown in the area. Currently 80% of the population of Kuala Gula are of Chinese ethnicity.

- In 1970, the Department of Wildlife and National Parks/ PERHILITAN and Perak State designated the area of Kuala Gula as a bird sanctuary.
- Between 2003 and 2005, an Environmental NGO (Wetlands International – Malaysia Programme) started a project nominating Kuala Gula as a second Ramsar Site for Malaysia, which included elements to educate locals to become ecotourism guides in the Malay and Chinese communities in Kuala Gula.
- After completion of the two-year project, in 2006 the Global Environment Centre, a new NGO, started a new project focusing on mangrove rehabilitation, mainly with Malay community members. Originally, the plan was for fishers to earn sufficient income from the mangrove rehabilitation and ecotourism projects that they no longer needed to fish.
- The Friends of the Mangrove's (40 residents from the Malay community, mostly fishers) activity included: growing saplings and selling them to tourists and schools to plant; renting out their fishing boats for mangrove planting; surveillance for illegal cutting of mangrove trees; providing educational activities to young people.
- 'The Friends' hold around 20,000 young mangrove trees all year round in the nursery, aiming to plant 1,000 per month. Usually they try to cover 2–8 ha of planting per year. Since the activity started, around 1,300 students, government officials and citizens have planted 50,000 mangrove saplings in the rehabilitation site. The support group included an NGO (Global Environment Centre); the Ministry of Nature Resources and Environment; the Forestry Department of Peninsular Malaysia; Perak State Forest Department; Force of Nature Aid Foundation (FON); CIMB Foundation; and the Department of Wildlife and National Parks.
- The tidal flat and the mangrove area of Kuala Gula is also known as a place where various species of migratory and resident birds stopover and feed and has been identified as one of the 10 most important ecotourism sites in Perak State. Tourists who visit the area come from around the country and abroad, for example Singapore; many also visit Penang, the nearby World Heritage Site.

Table B.2 Communities within Kuala Gula

	Chinese A	Chinese B	Malay C	Plantation D		Chinese E
Community 集落	Taman Muhibbah タマン ムヒバ	Bagan Cina バガンチナ	PSKT (Malay) PSKT マレー	Ladang Gula (Eng Thye Plantation) ラダングラ (アンタイ・プランテーション)	Ladang Chersonese (Sime & Durby Plantation) ラダンチェソニー (サイム&ダービープランテーション)	Bagan Seberang バガン スプラン
Main ethnicity 主なエスニシティー	Chinese 中華系	Chinese 中華系	Malay マレー系	Private Chinese company (Singaporean ownership) with local and international workers 中華系会社(シンガポールに所有者・地域及び海外からの労働者)	Government-link Malaysian company with local and international workers 政府関連のマレー系会社・地域及び海外からの労働者	Chinese 中華系
Main industry 主な産業	Fishery (shrimps, shellfish) 漁業(えび・赤貝)	Fishery (shrimps, shellfish) 漁業(えび・赤貝)	Fishery (crabs and fish) 漁業(カニ・魚)	Palm oil plantation パーム プランテーション	Palm oil plantation パーム プランテーション	Fishery (shrimps, shellfish) and tourism industry with seafood 漁業(えび・赤貝)と海鮮料理を中心とした観光業
Geography 地理	River mouth (Gula River) 河口(グラ川)	River mouth 河口	River mouth 河口	Inland 内陸	Inland 内陸	Different river mouth (Kurau River) 別の河口(クラウ川)
Estimated population 推定人口	3, 800		770	400	400	1, 000
% of the population in Kuala Gula village 人口割合	59. 6%		12. 1%	6. 3%	6. 3%	15. 7%
Survey numbers being collected (out of 81) 質問票 収集数(計81)	48		10	5	5	13
Distance from the mangrove rehabilitation site 再生サイトからの距離	Close 近い →					Far (15 km radius) 遠い(周囲15キロ)

Name of the place 場所	Kuala Gula, Kerian District, Perak, Malaysia マレーシア・ペラ州クリアン郡クアラグラ村
Size of the area for the mangrove rehabilitation project 再生事業面積	608 hectare 608ヘクタール
Current status of the project 再生事業の進展状況	Project is ongoing. In 2006 when the sea wall was naturally breached, the local fishermen started to replant the mangroves, which were cut down for village settlements. 集落を造成するためにマングローブ林が伐採され干拓が行われたが、堤防が自然決壊。2006年より、その場所に近隣漁民によってマングローブの植林が継続中
Aim of the project 事業目的	Rehabilitation of oceanic biodiversity, prevention of tsunami disasters, creation of environmental education site, creation of community managed forest site, turning planting activities into a tourist attraction 海洋生態系回復、津波防災対策、環境教育サイト作り、集落が管理する森林作り、植林活動を観光のアトラクションに

Local and tourism resources in Kuala Gula

- Mangrove plantation activities (for education and 'cooperate social responsibility' activities)
- Bird watching (Ramsar candidate site)
- Observing mammals, including otters
- Resort hotel by the river mouth (run by the government)
- Wildlife (migratory bird) museum (in the Department of Wildlife and National Parks office)
- Matang Mangrove Forest: the biggest mangrove habitat on the Malay Peninsula. A 50 km stretch along the tidal flat area of the west coast of the north part of Perak state, with 40 km beside five river mouths in the protected area. In September to March, more than 20,000 migratory birds, comprising 50 species use the area as a feeding ground
- Fish, prawns and mud crabs (also called soft-shell crab or shedding crab) are caught in the mangrove forests, and large-scale farming of blood cockles on the tidal flats
- Sembilang are fish with a reputation for having a 'clean taste' due to their mangrove habitat
- Dried shrimps and belacan (shrimp cooking paste)

5 Local power through the Mangrove Rehabilitation Project in Kuala Gula, Malaysia

Balu Perumal, Alifah Ilyana Binti Mohd Husni and Amirah Adibah Binti Adenan

5.1 Mangrove restoration in Malaysia: The context

Malaysia has some 4,800 km of coastline, half formed of sandy beaches, with some mangroves and the rest rocky shores (Teh, 2001). Mangrove forests grow on the marine alluvium along sheltered coasts and estuaries. They are found on the west coast of Peninsular Malaysia in the states of Perak, Selangor and Johore; along the east coast of Sabah; and in northern and southwestern Sarawak. There are approximately 642,400 ha of mangrove forest in Malaysia, 17% in Peninsular Malaysia, 57% in Sabah and 26% in Sarawak.

Mangrove forests provide many ecological services, including coastal protection, energy conversion, nutrient trapping and recycling, and support of fish stocks etc. Mangroves are also of great socio-economic importance, supporting commercial fish and prawn industries, sustainable timber production and providing various products used by local communities. Approximately 446,000 ha of these mangroves have been designated as forest reserves, which come under the jurisdiction of the respective State Forestry Departments and are considered protected and well managed. Those outside these areas, however, have been greatly reduced and disturbed due to reclamation activities for agriculture, residential and resort development, clearance for aquaculture, wood chipping (in Sarawak) and exploitation of other non-sustainable activities. According to Richards and Friess (2016), Malaysia lost 2.83% of its mangroves between the years 2000 and 2012, of which 38.2% was for agriculture, 14.7% for aquaculture and 12.8% for urban development.

Despite this, Malaysia has much experience managing mangrove forests; the 40,000 ha Matang Mangroves are arguably one of the world's best managed regarding forestry use (Watson, 1928; Ong, 1982; Chan, 2001; Gan, 1995; Azahar and Nik Mohd Shah, 2003). The management system here includes replanting areas after harvesting where

DOI: 10.4324/9780367863098-5

natural regeneration is inadequate. However, this restoration is confined almost entirely to just two commercial species, *Rhizophora apiculata* and *Rhizophora mucronata.* Local communities' involvement in mangrove forest management has been minimal and restricted to fishery activities, despite them being identified as the main stakeholders in and impacted by the degradation of the mangrove forest.

These local communities, mainly fishers and paddy farmers, are self-employed and of poor economic standing. They use thc mangrove forest as their daily source of wood. However, high demand for mangrove trees for charcoal and construction industries has also contributed to the illegal extraction of mangrove trees. There is genuine concern that due to the reduction in and degradation of the mangrove forest, the community face increasing problems of displacement and disruption of their daily activities, including loss of livelihoods, as consequences of coastal erosion, frequent flooding and loss of mangrove resources. Thus, it is not surprising that local communities have been identified as the 'missing link' with regard to the Mangrove Rehabilitation Project initiated by the government. In this chapter, 'restoration' and 'rehabilitation' are used interchangeably.

Malaysia was affected by the 2004 Indian Ocean earthquake, which was followed by the devastating tsunami on 26 December 2004. Although located close to the epicentre, it was shielded from the initial impact by the island of Sumatra and was only impacted by reflected waves. Nevertheless, the northwest coastline of Peninsular Malaysia was affected most by the disaster. The death toll was 67, and more than 8,000 people residing along the coastline were badly affected, either made homeless or had their livelihoods disrupted. The most common issues reported following this tsunami were damage to houses, fishing boats, equipment and assets related to fisheries, and agricultural projects. However, certain areas near the shoreline in parts of the states of Perlis, Kedah and Perak were effectively protected from serious damage by tidal mangroves, which formed a natural coastal protection structure.

Many studies were subsequently conducted along the impacted coastline; one of the authors of this chapter (then working with the Global Environment Centre) was involved in assessment of the Perak mangroves, conducted in the fourth quarter of 2005. The objectives of the survey were to assess the impact of the tsunami on the coastal environment and identify potential areas where mangrove restoration could be carried out with the local communities. The results from the assessment were presented to the national government for consideration. Together with other studies, the tsunami impact and recovery programme was discussed in a wider consultative forum at the National Coastal Tree Replanting Committee established by the Malaysian Government after the 2004 Indian Ocean tsunami.

The Ministry of Natural Resources and Environment, who chaired the committee, accepted the idea and endorsed its implementation saying local community activity would be facilitated by the non-governmental organisations (NGOs). Thus, for the first time in Malaysian history, local communities were actively involved in a national programme on mangrove protection and restoration. Subsequently, the government (through the Prime Minister's Department) also allocated some RM25 million within the 5-year Malaysia Plans (2006–2020) to rehabilitate about 4,000 ha of mangroves with a target of planting 50 million mangrove trees in the aftermath of the tsunami.

About seven NGOs were involved in the national coastal tree planting programme; for example, the Malaysian Nature Society, Penang Inshore Fisheries Welfare Association, World Wide Fund for Nature Malaysia and Wetlands International Malaysia Programme. The Mangrove Rehabilitation Project at Kuala Gula was spearheaded by the Global Environment Centre (GEC). It was hoped that through such a community programme, the number of citizens dependent on the mangroves as a source of income through destructive means could be minimised and the value of the ecosystem appreciated.

5.2 The Mangrove Rehabilitation Project in Kuala Gula, Perak

In Kuala Gula, the restoration activities with local community groups focused on an abandoned village settlement known as Teluk Rubiah, a large tract of mangrove forest reclaimed in the mid-1960s. In 1970, the Department of Wildlife and National Parks set up an office base there and together with the Perak State government, worked towards designating Kuala Gula as a bird sanctuary. Under this initiative, between 2003 and 2005, an environmental NGO (Wetlands International, Malaysia Programme) started a project nominating Kuala Gula as a second Ramsar Site for Malaysia, which included training locals as ecotourism guides in Kuala Gula. The lead author was then the project leader. After the two-year project was completed, he moved to work with another NGO, the Global Environment Centre, remaining at the same site but focusing on mangrove restoration, mainly with Malay community members.

Sahabat Hutan Bakau (SHB) or 'Friends of the Mangrove' (40 residents consisting mostly of fishers) was established as a result. Their activity included growing mangrove saplings and selling them to tourists to plant; renting out their fishing boats for mangrove planting and bird watching; surveillance for illegal activities in the mangroves; and providing educational activities to school students.

Their involvement in the Mangrove Rehabilitation Project was equally motivated by awareness and concern for the local environment, which supports their livelihood as fishers. The importance of using local knowledge in the conservation and sustainable management of this ecosystem was also key in this local approach. At the start of the programme, numerous stakeholder consultations were held with local people, community heads and government agencies on how to implement the community Mangrove Rehabilitation Project. SHB adopted four different methods for mangrove restoration, considering the local enabling conditions:

- Encourage natural mangrove restoration, that is, by allowing/simulating tidal flow into the abandoned Teluk Rubiah area
- Direct planting of mangrove propagules in areas with little exposure to strong waves
- Systematic planting techniques of raising saplings from mangrove nurseries and planting at an even distance, as adopted and applied by the Forestry Department
- Assisted planting of mangrove tree saplings in difficult areas (i.e. areas constantly exposed to wave action and/or in deep mud areas).

To facilitate the mangrove planting, SHB also established a mangrove nursery that could hold up to 20,000 mangrove saplings per year. This was to ensure a continuous supply for restoration activity. The choice of species was not restricted to commercial ones (i.e. Rhizophora spp.) but also included other species such as Avicennia spp., Sonneratia spp. and Bruguiera spp (Figure 5.1).

The activity was conducted on a monthly basis by SHB but was sometimes scaled up during special events and public holidays. Between 2007 and 2017, more than 100,000 saplings were planted involving more than 10,000 people from 250 groups. This was conducted in an area covering 100 ha of the Teluk Rubiah tidal flats and was a fun and meaningful way to involve the public and schools in the mangrove conservation programme. The response from the stakeholders and public was very encouraging. Many from the private sector and corporate social responsibility (CSR) stakeholders, including RICOH Malaysia, Shell Malaysia, the CIMB Foundation and Force of Nature Aid Foundation, provided financial support for SHB activities (Figure 5.2).

Figure 5.1 Planting locations of various mangrove species at Teluk Rubiah (Global Environment Centre).

5.3 Activities for livelihood development

Socio-economic considerations were an important component within the community project, aiming to provide sustained benefits to the participating communities. Opportunities for alternative income generation from mangrove restoration activities were tested during the

Figure 5.2 CSR groups' mangrove planting and educational activities (Global Environment Centre).

project period. Direct monetary benefits received through part-time employment; rental of boats; facilities and services; and on-going tree planting activities, including ecotourism etc. were considerable (RM200 to RM500/month/person) and encouraged the local community's voluntary participation in the programme. Naturally abundant resources in the area, like seashells, were made into high-end handicrafts and souvenirs, which generated alternative income for some coastal people (Figure 5.3).

5.4 Communication, education, participation and awareness (CEPA) programme

At Kuala Gula, the GEC worked closely with other NGOs, namely the Malaysian Nature Society (through their school nature clubs) and Penang Inshore Fisheries Welfare Association, to conduct CEPA activities and to engage local community participation and sustain their interest in the Mangrove Rehabilitation Project. They produced much information and educational material, and a dedicated social media site was created. Road shows, exhibitions and public events were also held in schools and nearby villages as part of an outreach programme. Outputs

Figure 5.3 Shell crafts made by Friends of the Mangrove members (Global Environment Centre).

and lessons learned from the project were shared with other communities and stakeholders at a national level, to enable them to initiate similar projects, which widened the impact.

The GEC also established a mangrove education centre at Kuala Gula in 2007, with basic infrastructure consisting of a short observation platform and a nursery area. The site is managed by SHB and acts as an outdoor field station. It was a big success with school children and visitors alike, and contributed in terms of hands-on, experiential learning. Many schools came during the weekends to plant mangroves. Many camps were conducted by SHB with help from the GEC, where they acted as facilitators explaining mangrove ecology, the importance of protecting it and why they need to plant more mangroves. In the first five years, no less than 2,000 children, from both primary and secondary schools, and 200 teachers benefited from the education centre.

5.5 Community and environmental sustainability

Establishing collaborative management, with local communities being given significant roles and responsibilities, is vital. A grass-roots approach is usually most effective as local stakeholders are already quite aware of the importance of the mangrove ecosystem. The voices of the Kuala Gula community needed to be heard to protect the mangroves for their livelihoods and coastal protection; this would only be achievable through local community unity. This programme has helped to empower the community and make them more aware of how crucial it is for them to safeguard the mangroves for their livelihoods.

A sense of belonging among the SHB members has developed, and they are more proactive in the Mangrove Rehabilitation Project activities. An air of positivity emanates from SHB and their success stories have induced other communities to start caring for their mangrove forests. SHB has since been invited to share their knowledge and experience with many communities, and in 2010 they were formally registered as a community-based organisation under the Registry of Societies of Malaysia. They now stand tall and work independently of the GEC.

5.6 Kuala Gula as a protected site

Kuala Gula is a well-known stopover and feeding ground for thousands of migratory birds (48 species and 8 families) using the East Asia Australian Flyway during the wintering season. Here both humans and birds depend on the tidal flat and mangrove ecosystem for their survival. Recognising this, in 2003 the federal government first made known its intention to protect the Kuala Gula wetlands as the second Ramsar site for Malaysia. The initiative was supported by Wetlands International Malaysia Programme through a DANIDA project (2003–2005) but did not find any traction with the Perak State Government and the plan was soon dropped. However, in 2017 more than 10 years into SHB and the GEC's Mangrove Rehabilitation Project, the Perak State Government finally designated the site at Teluk Rubiah as a new forest reserve (The STAR, 20 June 2014). They intend that it will be co-managed as a community forest, the first in the state and among a handful within the country.

5.7 Conclusion: Implications for future practice and research needs

In terms of the ladder of participation for citizens, the Kuala Gula case showed that even though a project originally starts off with 'authorities-initiated' decision making, it can become 'citizen-initiated' using people's initiatives and ideas as a result of experiencing many small successes. Rural villages have their own particular ways of decision making, and how the project can be a part of their decision making processes is crucial. Several lessons have been derived from the community-led Mangrove Rehabilitation Project that we would like to share.

5.7.1 A village committee and community support for making projects successful

Realistically, a lot of investment has gone into this project. For example, the lead author spent close to 10 years working at the location to gain local trust; the first three years with Wetlands International Malaysia Programme (2003–2005) then seven years with the GEC (2006–2012). Since there are six different communities in Kuala Gula, all had to be visited, introduced to the project and consulted with in an elaborate stakeholder engagement process. This allows one to understand the power and political play in the village settings, including the interest they might have in the project.

From all the exercises conducted, we found the Malay community more amenable to involvement in the project because they are mostly self-employed (fishers), have more control over their time and find the project activities help improve their income significantly. Comparatively, the Chinese community are very industrious, busy and economically stable; the Indian community are not free to participate since most are employed as plantation workers. Nevertheless, the benefits of the project were made accessible to all, especially in terms of capacity building, education and ecotourism opportunities. Friends of the Mangrove was created as a non-political platform to represent the local community interest group keen to take on the responsibility of managing the environment; this directly reports to the village committee. They also liaise with citizens, NGOs and the government in matters relating to the Mangrove Rehabilitation Project.

5.7.2 Strong partnerships to enhance the scale and scope of mangrove restoration

This was especially true during the early days of the project; the early buy-ins surprisingly came from schools and the local authorities wanting such projects. First, as part of an alternative/experiential learning and awareness programme for the public, and second and more importantly, to solve local socio-economic teething problems compounded by mangrove destruction (e.g. low fish catches and illegal activities related to the forest).

The Mangrove Rehabilitation Project flourished with their continuous presence and support, which was often conducted on a weekly or monthly basis. The Malaysian Nature Society were especially helpful in bringing in school groups, which led to the establishment of the mangrove education centre. The educational visits or study trip activities were later expanded to engage the general public through ecotourism packages. Next came the partnership with the Forest Research Institute Malaysia and Mangrove Action Project, who provided basic training to the local community on mangrove restoration and introduced innovative ways of rehabilitating large areas by incorporating hydrological restoration techniques. Engagement, mobilisation and training have definitely empowered the local communities involved in the Mangrove Rehabilitation Project. Participation of various specialist groups, on the other hand, has enhanced the scale and scope of the mangrove restoration.

5.7.3 Importance of counterpart funding

Counter funding should be mobilised from partner organisations, local government and communities to maximise resources and underpin the collaborative approach to restoration projects. Under the national Mangrove Rehabilitation Project, the Ministry (MNRE) has been a sustained funding source, albeit on a year-to-year basis, for the community activities. The GEC also has been resourceful in seeking CSR funding from various sources. In addition, the 'pay and plant' concept has been incorporated within tourism packages, which were promoted and have attracted various interest groups.

Initially, opportunities for alternative income was a main reason in keeping the community interested and engaged. Direct monetary benefits were considerable and encouraged the local community's voluntary participation in the programme. In the long run, however, community appreciation and recognition of the importance of their mangrove resources to their livelihoods has prevailed. Their contribution of labour then became the basis for ownership – very much evident in the increased fish catches, the forest they helped create and the role that they created for themselves as mangrove protectors.

5.7.4 Using tenurial instruments

Tenurial instruments, such as the community-based forest managed areas, can be used to sustain community initiatives in the long term. If Kuala Gula is to be managed as part of a large contiguously managed mangrove ecosystem (with Larut Matang FRs) in Peninsular Malaysia and accorded the Ramsar site designation, it can become an internationally recognised example of collaborative management of a mangrove ecosystem. This can occur with provision for sustainable financing for more effective management in the area, in tandem with a broad range of programmes supporting tenure rights, poverty reduction and sustainable socio-economic development.

Other implications for future practice include the following:

- There is a need to strengthen the information, education and communication programmes for the protection and conservation of degraded mangrove areas.
- The local community needs to be engaged in the management of mangrove forests and their resources as a more sustainable approach. They must be given technical assistance, training, education and diverse livelihood programmes to enhance their capability to contribute more effectively to forest management.
- Successful projects always start with proper awareness and trust built with the local community. Therefore, there is a need for more engaging activities and an awareness campaign on the ecological and socio-economic importance of mangrove forests.

5.7.5 ***Future research needs***

There is a great need for future conservation that integrates research, training, advocacy and action, including all sectors of society at all levels.

- There is a wealth of experience in mangrove reforestation, restoration and replanting in many countries (Hong 1994; Chan 1996; Primavera and Esteban 2008; Biswas et al. 2009) that can be used to help enhance adaptive capacity. Restoration of degraded mangrove systems is an effective strategy for building climate change resilience, particularly where sections of an otherwise healthy system are degraded.
- The Forestry Department need to involve the local community in the overall management of the mangrove forests. Local communities will acquire greater awareness and a shared responsibility, as well as benefit financially by co-managing the resources, acting accordingly to help conserve them.
- The diverse mangrove plants and animals and their adaptations make the mangrove ecosystem an ideal ecological destination and provide field laboratories for biology and ecology students and researchers.

References

Azahar, M. and Nik Mohd Shah, N.M. (2003) *A working plan of the Matang Mangrove forest reserves, Perak: The third 10-year period (2000–2009) of the second rotation.* Perak Darul Ridzuan, Malaysia: State Forestry Department of Perak, p.320.

Biswas S.R., Mallik A.U., Choudhury J.K. and Nishat A. (2009) A united framework for the restoration of Southeast Asian mangroves: Bridging ecology, society, and economics. *Wetlands Ecology and Management.* 17, 365–383.

Chan, H.T. (1996) *Mangrove reforestation in Peninsular Malaysia.* In: Field, C.D. (ed), *Restoration of mangrove ecosystems.* Okinawa, Japan: International Society for Mangrove Ecosystems, pp. 64–75.

Chan, H.T. (2001) 'The Matang mangroves.' In: Ong, J.E. and Gong, W.K. (eds.), *Encyclopedia of Malaysia, Vol. 6, The Seas.* Editions Didier Millet. Singapore: Archipelago Press, pp.130–131.

Gan, B.K. (1995) A working plan for the Matang Mangrove Forest Reserve, Perak. Fourth Revision. Perak Darul Ridzuan, Malaysia: State Forestry Department of Perak, p. 214.

Hong, P.N. (1994) 'Reafforestation of mangrove forests in Vietnam'. In *Proceedings of an International Timber Organisation Workshop: Development and Dissemination of Reafforestation Techniques of Mangrove Forests.* Japanese Association for Mangroves, Okinawa, pp. 141–165.

Ong, J.E. (1982) 'Aquaculture, forestry and conservation of Malaysian mangroves.' *Ambio,* 11, 252–257.

Primavera, J.H. and Esteban, J.M.A. (2008) 'A review of mangrove rehabilitation in the Philippines: Successes, failures and future prospects.' *Wetlands Ecology and Management*, 16(3), 173–253.

Richards, D.R., and Friess, D.A. (2016) 'Rates and drivers of mangrove deforestation in Southeast Asia, 2000-2012.' *Proceedings of the National Academy of Sciences USA*, 113, 344–349.

Teh, T.S. (2001) 'Coastlines.' In: Ong, J.E. and Gong, W.K. (eds.) *Encyclopedia of Malaysia, Vol. 6, The Seas.* Editions Didier Millet. Singapore: Archipelago Press, pp. 38–39.

The Star, 20 Jun 2014. 'Protecting Kuala Gula'. Accessed October 27, 2020 at: https://www.thestar.com.my/news/community/2014/06/20/protecting-kuala-gula-gazetting-mangrove-for-rehabilitation-and-reforestation.

Watson, J.G. (1928) *Mangrove forests of the Malay Peninsula.* Malayan Forest Records 6. Singapore: Fraser & Neave, pp. 1–275.

6 Community perceptions towards the risks and benefits of a mangrove restoration project

Learning from a case study in Malaysia

Hiromi Yamashita and Naoyuki Mikami

6.1 Background of the Mangrove Rehabilitation Project in Kuala Gula, Malaysia

As discussed in the previous chapter, in Kuala Gula mangrove forests were cut down in the 1960s to create reclaimed land by drainage for village settlements. The newly created land suffered from continuous flooding from the sea as the sea walls were naturally breached many times and the government gave up repairing them. In 1970, the Department of Wildlife and National Parks (PERHILITAN) and Perak State designated the area of Kuala Gula as a bird sanctuary. Between 2003 and 2005, an environmental non-governmental organisation (NGO) (Wetlands International – Malaysia Programme) started a project nominating Kuala Gula as a second Ramsar Site for Malaysia, which included training locals to become ecotourism guides in the Malay and Chinese communities in Kuala Gula.

Almost 90% of the Malay villagers are said to be involved in fishing or related industries, especially around specific fish, shrimp, cockles and crabs. The local specialties are soft-shell crab; belacan (shrimp cooking paste); and traditional catfish. These delicacies are served either at a Malay floating restaurant or in local Chinese restaurants. Chinese communities near this Malay settlement operate ecotourism, mainly taking Chinese tourists from Singapore or nearby Asian countries to observe mangrove replanting and eat these local delicacies. Although the Malay and Chinese communities operate tours separately, they communicate and work together to accommodate and transport guests coming into the community.

DOI: 10.4324/9780367863098-6

6.2 Research methods

This study hoped to give insights into the types and depth of people's perceptions towards restoration projects, and some thoughts for effective environmental communication and decision making for the future. We have employed two main research methods.

6.2.1 Stakeholder interviews over 3.5 years

We hoped to collect a variety of information on the project, provided by different stakeholders. 15 people were interviewed in November 2013 in the village, and the interviews normally lasted more than an hour. We wanted to know what kinds of attempts the interviewees made to obtain public support for this restoration project, and what they have observed in terms of changing people's perceptions of risks and benefits towards the project over the years.

In March 2017, about three and half years after the first survey, we tried to contact the 15 interviewees on site again to identify any perception change. We succeeded in conducting 10 follow-up interviews. On the basis of these two waves of interviews, we planned a questionnaire survey of general populations of different communities close to the Mangrove Rehabilitation Project site (i.e., the Malay fishing community, the Chinese tourism industry and Indian and Chinese plantation communities).

6.2.2 Questionnaire data from 81 randomly sampled respondents

The questionnaire was conducted between 14 and 19 September 2017 in all the constituency villages. The questionnaire survey targeted people older than 15 years who lived in Kuala Gula. Randomly selected respondents were visited at their home, and their answers were collected either by a structured interview method (the researcher fills out the questionnaire for the respondent) or a distribution survey method (the researcher watches the respondent fill in the questionnaire). Since it was not possible to conduct a random sampling of the respondents by using tools such as a basic resident register (information about all the residents in the area), the research team chose the second best way by randomly choosing the data collection starting points on the village maps (see details in Appendix 1). We obtained 81 responses from all six constituency villages.

The questionnaire format was created in English first, then translated into Malay and Chinese. Which form was used depended on the language the respondent preferred. The questionnaire consisted of the following areas with 22 questions in total: (1) change of coastal environment; image of mangroves and tidal flats, understanding of their functions; (2) awareness of reclaimed land by drainage; (3) awareness of and opinions towards the Mangrove Rehabilitation Project; (4) indicators of the success of the rehabilitation project; (5) citizens' participation; (6) opinions and suggestions for mangrove rehabilitation projects; and (7) information about respondents (including gender, age group, nationality, ethnicity, length of stay in Kuala Gula, occupation).

6.3 Findings

Here we will look at the results from the interviews and the questionnaire to understand local people's perceptions towards the restoration project.

6.3.1 Perceived benefits of the restoration project

When the initial interviews were conducted in 2013, interviewees' perceptions on the benefits of the project were as follows: increase in fish stocks (crab, shrimps and fish); fish prices go up since it is well known as a clean area (raised self-confidence in the area), attracting more birds; fresh seafood to treat visitors, creating tourism and other income sources (wider choice of lifestyles), self-confidence raised by meeting people, providing young people with educational opportunities and preventing tsunamis (Table 6.1).

The questionnaire results tell us that the common reasons people chose to promote the Mangrove Rehabilitation Project were: reduction of natural disasters (80.0%); returning land to the sea (76.9%, "because it is ideal that we return it to the ocean since it was originally part of the sea"); gaining visitor attractions (73.8%); boosting the local image (73.8%); and raising seafood production (72.3%). It was interesting that people at the palm oil plantations, which are inland, also saw the benefits of the project since either their companies were also promoting mangrove rehabilitation activities, or they went out sea fishing nearby.

6.3.2 Challenges and risks perceived by the neighbouring residents

During the interview process, aspects of risk were rarely mentioned by the interviewees in Kuala Gula, apart from one opinion, which was that the project is promoting the 'wrong' way of planting mangroves, with little biological understanding of mangroves. The respondent knew

Table 6.1 Benefits identified by the interviewees in Kuala Gula

National/Global	• Increase in fish stocks (crab, shrimp and fish) • Nature conservation for migratory birds
Local	• Increase in fish stocks • Attracting more birds for tourism • Developing tourism as another income source • Disaster risk reduction from future tsunamis • Increasing pride in their community • Providing young people with educational opportunities • Cohesion between the different communities by working towards the same goal (especially among the Chinese and Malay communities, and to a lesser extent with the Indian community)
Personal	• Increase in fish stock • New source of income • Pride in their occupations and being fishers • Self-development and business training opportunities (e.g. being efficient, time management, developing communication skills by meeting new people) • Creating chances for people who left for the cities to return ('we can save more money by living here') • Widening lifestyle choices (e.g. where they live, what they do)

about hydrology, and which trees like drier or wetter environments; however, when asked if he had communicated this to the people planting the mangrove trees, he said he had not.

In the questionnaire, only two people stated that the Mangrove Rehabilitation Project should not be promoted. The reasons were "because local people are not interested in it" and "because it does not attract many people to visit from outside of the area". There were no criticisms of the Mangrove Rehabilitation Project itself. Rather, there were strong requests from other communities to get involved in the project in the questionnaire data. This is positive for the project but at the same time, it could be a cause of jealousy in the future if active involvement was limited to members from one Malay community only.

6.3.3 Changes of perceptions towards the benefits of the process

Restoration projects take time, during which the purpose and meaning of the project itself as well as how people see the project changes (see Table 6.2). The research project wanted to find out how people perceived the risks and benefits of the restoration (at one particular time). The activity might not change, but the purpose of the project and

Table 6.2 Changes of local perceptions towards the project from 2013 to 2017 (about 3.5 years)

Elements of change	*Nov. 2013*	*March 2017*	*Perception changes observed*
Positive impact of the restoration activities	"This project is changing the local environment for the better"	"Perhaps the project does not have much influence on the environment"	Positive impacts of the project which were felt strongly in 2013 were not felt directly in 2017. The negative influence seemed to stem from the new government-backed shrimp farm that opened nearby. It cut down pristine mangrove forests, and pumped "polluted" water out to the ocean
Perceptions towards coastal environment	"Getting better" due to the restoration project"	"Getting worse"; "much more competition among fishers than before"	
Income from the ecotourism activities	"Increasing"	"Decreasing"	Nearby cities started to copy mangrove planting ecotourism activities (new competitors)
Activities preferred in the fishing community	Choosing to contribute to the restoration activities, sometimes over fishing activities	Choosing fishing more than restoration activities	In 2013, the restoration activity payment (around 50RM) compensated for the loss of fishing income. However, in 2017 a day's fishing pays more (100 RM) than the restoration payment (50RM).

environmental circumstances might change over time. The interviews identified that the following elements seem to have influenced how people perceive the risks and benefits of the restoration project in Kuala Gula.

In the north part of the village, a new intensive shrimp farm was built through a public/private partnership. For this project, 250 ha of mangrove forest were cleared, and the villagers complained that polluted water was being discharged into the nearby river channel. Some people expressed confusion about the government's tactics by saying, "why do they encourage mangrove restoration, while at the same time chop down the trees just next door?" Also, to the south, a new village started conducting mangrove planting tourism in competition. Kuala Gula became a victim of its own success.

There are three types of uncertainties exist in environmental issues: uncertainty of what will happen; uncertainty of who will receive risks/benefits and what will they be; and uncertainty about the predictions (whether risks will actually happen or not, or when). In this case study, the benefits of planting mangroves, or in other words, the harmful effects of not planting mangroves, seem to be 'certain' in people's mind. However, the uncertainties of who receives what kinds of risks/benefits makes the base of the project unstable. At the same time, it is hard to make a judgment about how long one needs to wait to see the direct benefits from a project. The restoration activities, including planting mangroves, remain but the benefits of mangrove planting became 'invisible' or 'unfelt' due to the nearby development.

6.3.4 Levels of enthusiasm for the project across different villages

Despite strong support for the mangrove restoration activities in general, nearly half of the respondents in the questionnaire answered that they had never heard about the mangrove restoration project conducted by the residents' group since 2006 (47%). About 90% of the residents in the Malay community, which hosts the mangrove restoration project, knew about it. Meanwhile, in the Chinese community, which is close to the restoration site, 64% of the residents answered that they had 'never heard' about the project, as well as around 60% of the respondents in the plantation communities. Of the respondents, 80.2% thought the Mangrove Rehabilitation Project should be promoted, with 54.3% thinking the project should be promoted 'strongly'. So, it is a shame they did not know the project existed right on their doorstep.

Different levels of acknowledgement were felt across different communities (Malay, Chinese, plantations). This might be because in Kuala Gula living areas and public facilities including schools, newspapers, shops and restaurants are separated according to language (Malay, Chinese, Hindu and others) and religion. Although the mangrove restoration projects appear in the national press, not all communities may have accessed the information. Different communities approach mangrove restoration tourism in different ways (Table 6.3).

Even in the same district, perceptions towards the coastal environment and the Mangrove Rehabilitation Project vary from small community to small community. How the community interact with the environment day to day seems to mirror how the community show the mangroves to visitors. The different fishing methods these communities

Table 6.3 Ecotourism approaches taken by Malay and Chinese communities

Settlement	*Malay settlement*	*Chinese settlement*
Style of ecotourism	Practical learning on the restoration site on the mud and in the forests (raising saplings and asking visitors to buy them to plant; renting fishing boats to reach the restoration site)	Biological learning experience at a distance (not planting but taking visitors to watch others in forests or planting saplings)
Attraction	Main attraction is to have direct contact with restoration forests and activities	Main attraction is to eat local mangrove delicacies after the tour
Species the community catch and sell	Soft-shell crab living in the mangrove and catching fish for consumption in local and neighbouring cities; other fish and shellfish	Dry shrimp and shrimp paste, mainly for outside the local area and abroad; crab and other fish at their Chinese restaurants

use are also influencing how they see the mangroves. Malay communities who fish in mangrove forests seem to have noticed in detail the changes in the mangrove forests.

The ecological functions of mangroves seem to be understood by most residents. In particular, the responses from the Malay community, who conduct the mangrove restoration activities, show all respondents understand the mangroves' functions. In comparison, the functions of the tidal flats are not well understood.

6.4 Discussion

In the Kuala Gula case, issues of uncertainty are not about the benefits themselves, but more about the 'invisibility' of the existing benefits. How can the project generate interest when the benefits (to the environment) are there, but suddenly become invisible? Future elements to be investigated include the following:

- How long can one wait to see real benefits? (How long would people remain happy while benefits are not yet tangible?)
- While the benefits are not felt by fishers, how difficult would it become for them to promote the activities?

Due to the nearby developments causing negative impacts on the sea, within the mangrove restoration volunteer group there were a couple of people who felt the group should tackle outside issues directly and be more confrontational. While it is hard to feel the direct benefits, one thing that could be done is obtaining very local (onsite) data, away from the polluted area, to observe small environmental improvements, encouraging volunteers and community members and reaffirming their activities.

6.5 Conclusion: Implication for future practice and research needs

6.5.1 Implication for future practice

- Perceptions towards the coastal environment and Mangrove Rehabilitation Project vary from community to community. This might depend on what kind of fishing methods each community or respondent specialises in, or the relationships they have with mangroves in their day-to-day lives (e.g., whether they get close to the mangrove restoration areas for fishing to observe the changes).
- Images of mangroves are generally positive, and most respondents stated that restoration activities should be promoted. However, the image of tidal flats remains negative.
- The ecological functions of mangroves seem to be understood by most residents, especially those who are close to the mangroves for their work.
- Mangrove ecosystems are well recognised, while those of tidal flats are little known.
- Identify different communication flows within the different communities in one project constituency, and endeavour to let all residents know that restoration projects are ongoing, through different languages and public spaces.

6.5.2 Research needs

- Comparative studies on how different groups within the same community interact with their wetlands, and how their experience and knowledge does or does not influence local decision making.

Case Study C information for Chapters 7, 8 and 9

Ago Bay Tidal Flat Restoration Projects, Shima City, Mie Prefecture, Japan

Hiromi Yamashita, Naoyuki Mikami, Hideto Uranaka, and Hideki Kokubu

Project Summary

In Ago bay, four unique managed realignment projects were initiated by the local municipal and prefectural governments. As the first such restoration in the country, the projects tackled various administrative barriers, with no blueprint to follow. Through research in the local bay, the government officials, fishers and researchers made great personal efforts to repeatedly visit landowners of the sites, as well as those of the surrounding areas. They were remarkable in identifying their own local rules and agreements to make these restorations possible. However, there is still little direct involvement of local people in the restoration projects. This is despite strong support for these activities among citizens, especially with generations who remember having happy times at tidal flats collecting clams and catching fish.

Figure C.1 Shima City from the sky.

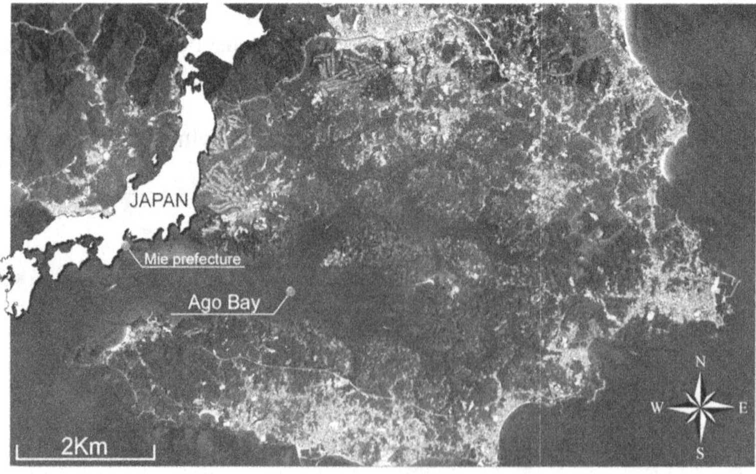

Figure C.2 Geographical features of Ago Bay: Area 26 km^2, Coastline 140 km; max depth 40 m, Bay mouth 12 m, width of Bay mouth, 1.7 km.

Source: Shima City.

Restoration Project Information

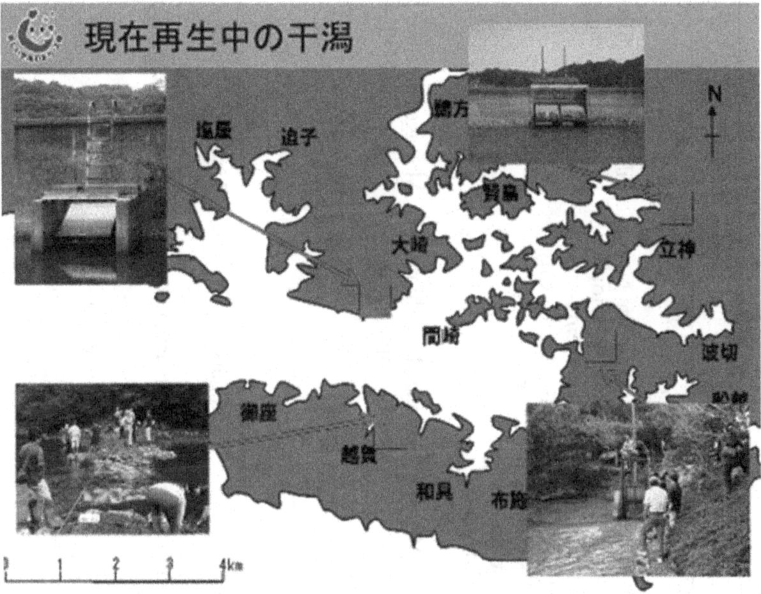

Figure C.3 The four restoration sites in Shima City.
Source: Urakana, 2018

Area Background

Shima City has one of the most iconic sceneries in Japan, especially when you observe it from the sky: many verdant islands with intricate ria coastlines dotted across Ago Bay, numerous rafts cultivating oysters and small fishing and tourist boats moving around the area. The world's cultured pearl industry started in Ago Bay, and now pearls are one of the most popular kinds of natural jewellery across the world.

In Ago Bay, the large quantity of akoya shells, which nurture pearls, and oyster shells have polluted the seabed with their faeces. Fishers also used to throw debris scraped from shells and oysters into the sea while they worked. This then provided food for bacteria and benthic organisms that consumed large amounts of oxygen. This created extremely low oxygen levels in the water (hypoxia), which then killed all kinds of living creatures in the ocean. Today, aosa seaweed production on the tidal flats and in shallow areas of water is taking over from pearl production in Ago Bay. However, domestic wastewater also seems to

Table C.1 Details of the Shima City tidal flat restoration projects

	Project 1	*Project 2*	*Project 3*	*Project 4*
Site name	Ishibuchi	Otani-ura	Niu no ike	Wagu-ura
Location	Inlet in Ishibuchi district, Shima City, Japan	Inlet within the Miyako Resort Oku-Shima Aqua Forest Aqua Villa Hotel (previously called Hotel Kintstsu Aqua Villa Ise-Shima), Shima City, Japan	Inlet within the Nemu Resort (previously called Nemu-mo-Sato), Shima City, Japan	Inlet in Wagu district, Shima City, Japan
Project type	Managed realignment	Managed by the Ministry of Environment	Managed by Shima Municipal Office	Managed by Shima Municipal Office
Year implemented	2010	2012	2012	2016
Size (ha)	2 ha	1 ha	2 ha	0.5 ha
Habitat restored	Tidal flats	Tidal flats	Tidal flats	Tidal flats
Project aim	Restoration of tidal flats' water purification mechanisms, enhancing oceanic biodiversity, creation of an environmental education site			

Project contractors	Shima Municipal Office, Mie Prefecture, Mie Fisheries Research Institute	Ministry of Environment, Shima Municipal Office, Miyako Resort Oku-Shima Aqua Forest	Shima Municipal Office, Mie Fisheries Research Institute, Nenu Resort	Shima Municipal Office, Wagu residents' association
Landowner(s)	No landowner; however, the project obtained written permissions from the landowners of the surrounding land and the local fishery association	Hotel owned premises	Hotel owned premises	One landowner of the area registered as 'mixed land' (previously 'farm land'), permissions were also obtained from the four landowners of the surrounding land, fishers and pearl culture workers
Stakeholders	Citizens, fishers association, residents association, prefecture agricultural department, private companies and landowners nearby	Citizens, fishers association, residents association, prefecture agricultural department, tourist operators, local hotel	Citizens, fishers association, residents association, prefecture agricultural department, tourist operators, local hotel	Citizens, fishers association, residents association, prefecture agricultural department, landowners nearby

be affecting the health of the ocean, and harmful algae blooms and red tides are appearing in the bay.

Status of the Utilisation of Tidal Flats and Reclaimed Areas in Ago Bay

It is surprising that approximately 70% of former tidal flats in Ago Bay have been reclaimed as rice fields (paddies), with more than 85% of these now unused wetland or fallow fields (Kokubu and Yamada, 2011). As a result of reclamation and dyke construction, hypoxia and red tides occur every year in the inner part of the bay (Nakanishi et al., 2001). Therefore, it is important to improve these unused areas, restoring them to tidal flats to revive the coastal environment and ecosystem.

In 2010, reclaimed land was located all around Ago Bay along the coast. The utilisation status and characteristic appearance of these areas were surveyed in 2005 and 2010 (Kokubu et al., 2010). These indicated that in 2005, 0.84 km^2 of tidal flats existed, with estuarine tidal flats at 0.03 km^2 and foreshore tidal flats at 0.81 km^2. There were 1.76 km^2 of reclaimed areas, of which 41 sites (0.31 km^2) were still cultivating paddies in 2005. In 2010, paddy fields had decreased to 19 sites (0.23 km^2). Uncultivated areas included 463 sites (1.45 km^2) in 2005 and 485 sites (1.53 km^2) in 2010. Of these, about 25% were used for other purposes in 2005 and 2010. Most of these uncultivated areas were small (under 0.01 km^2). About 58% of the dike were made using bonded stone, and about 23% of them had problems with seawater intrusion onto the uncultivated areas. Ten dike were already damaged. Many reclaimed areas became wetlands or fallow fields due to socio-economic changes such as a decrease in demand for rice and depopulation of the area. The rate of these changes also increased between 2005 and 2010.

References

Kokubu, H., Okumira, H. and Matsuda, O. (2008) 'Historical changes in the tidal flat and its effects on benthos and sediment quality in Ago Bay.' *Journal of Japan Society on Water Environment*, 31(6), 305–311.

Kokubu, H. and Yamada, H. (2011) 'Evaluation of tidal flat restoration effect in the coastal unused reclaimed area by promoting tidal exchange in Ago Bay.' *Journal of Japan Society of Civil Engineers, Ser. B2 (Coastal Engineering)*, 67(2), I 956-I 960 (in Japanese).

Nakanishi, K., Masuda, T., Hata, N. and Yamagata, Y. (2001) 'Ago wan ni okeru teishitsu osen no genjyo to kinnen no shinko jyokyo' [Present status of sediment pollution in Ago Bay and its recent changes]. Mie Prefecture Fisheries Research Institute Report 10, 71-77. (with English Abstract)

7 The Ago Bay experience from a local government perspective

Hideto Uranaka

7.1 The beauty of Shima City

Shima City is a municipality of around 49,000 people (as of July 2020) located in Mie Prefecture, which lies almost at the mid-point of Japan's Pacific coast. It has a land area of 179 km^2, but due to its treelike ria topography, its coastline extends for 295 km, the ninth longest municipal coastline in the country (Ago Town, 2000; Daio Town, 1994; Hamashima Town, 1989; Shima Town, 2004). The waters along this extremely irregular coastline make for a rich fishing industry; the Fishermen's Cooperative Association holds fishing rights for an area of the sea totalling 145 km^2. A prominent characteristic of the local fishing industry is the pearl cultivation carried out in Ago Bay. In 1946, all of Shima City and part of the sea around it were included to form the Ise-Shima National Park. This protected the environment so that now its natural beauty and fisheries are tourism resources, with tourism one of the economic mainstays of the community. The value of Shima's total production for 2011 was $880 million (Figure 7.1).

There are three different marine environments in Shima City. Ago Bay, with its intricate rias shoreline, is the cradle of pearl cultivation technology. Today the bay is also used for sea kayaking and other forms of leisure activities. Three rivers flow into Matoya Bay, supplying rich nutrients from surrounding lush forests. These nutrients form the basis of the thriving industries of oyster and aosa seaweed cultivation. Along the Pacific coast, a rich assortment of fish and shellfish are caught throughout the year using a variety of fishing techniques, including fixed net, fill net, long line and pole-and-line. Shima City also has a long tradition of female divers, called 'ama', who harvest seafood. These marine environments have a symbiotic relationship with the mountainous areas that are full of evergreen hardwoods, including oaks. The mountains used to be a place where people could collect wood for fires and create

DOI: 10.4324/9780367863098-7

Figure 7.1 Professional development training on the tidal flat restoration project at the Miyako Resort Okushima Aqua Forest Hotel.
Source: Shima City, 2014.

charcoal, and even now, these rich forests provide nutrients to the sea, which contribute to the ocean's biodiversity.

7.2 Challenges and opportunities seized during population and environmental decline

Shima City's population peaked in 1955, gradually decreasing thereafter. Particularly in recent years, a low birth rate combined with people relocating out of the city has resulted in an ageing society with few children and a rapidly declining population. A downturn in economic activity is seen as one of the reasons for the decline in population (Statistics Bureau of Japan, 2015). While Ise-Shima National Park, in which Shima City is located, is recognised as one the country's foremost tourist destinations, the value produced has been trending downwards. Lower productivity and weak prices in primary sector industries are thought to stem from rising competition between tourist destinations

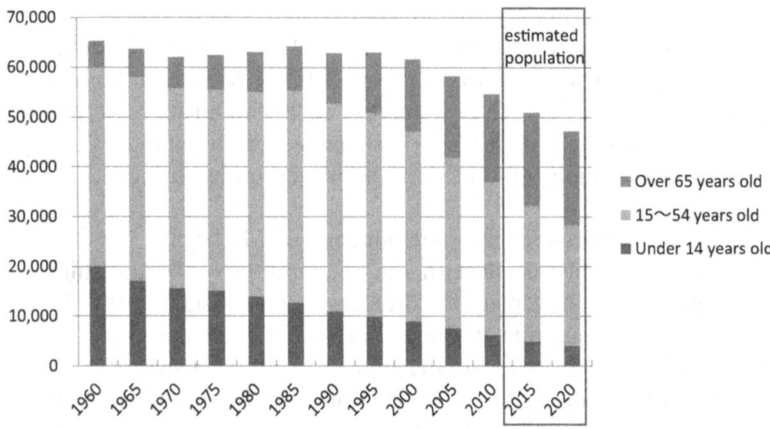

Figure 7.2 Changes in Shima City's population.
Source: the Statistics Bureau of Japan, 2015.

and economic sluggishness in tertiary industries, which are dominated by tourism.

Given its location within a national park, there is a call for Shima City to pursue economic growth through effective use of the area's natural resources rather than through large-scale development. Instead of attempting to harmonise large economic development with the natural environment, the city's economic activities reflect its integrated coastal management approach (ICM), which is based on how to best conserve and properly value nature's bounty in the midst of a population and economic downturn (Figure 7.2).

Fishing was Shima's primary industry in the 1960s. As tourism increased in the area, it was able to market marine products such as lobster, abalone and pearls as part of this developing industry. As such, it has long been engaged in initiatives for marine resource management and fishing ground habitat conservation aimed at promoting the fishing industry.

As Ago Bay has been used for pearl cultivation for many years, the seabed has accumulated excess nutrients from the pearl oysters' faecal waste and shells. This has been compounded by additional nutrients being added by fishers scraping the surface of the shells while at sea as part of the pearl cultivation and cleaning processes. To stop eutrophication, wastewater treatment and dredging of the organic matter that has accumulated on the sea floor has been carried out in the bay to suppress hypoxia and red tides. However, while some progress was made in improving water quality, the problem of oxygen depletion remained. To address this, a comprehensive survey of Ago Bay, including the surrounding land, was carried out from 2003 to 2007, with the results applied to an 'ocean health examination' in 2009. During these efforts, the 'satoumi' creation concept took shape as a basic plan for the city, aimed at recreating a full and smooth nutrient cycle both on the land and in the sea.

In 2010, discussions on introducing ICM began within the Shima City administration with the cooperation of Partnerships in Environmental Management for the Seas of East Asia and the Ocean Policy Research Institute (OPRI). They recognised the necessity of raising the plan's priority to the highest comprehensive plan level, establishing a promotion section to implement ICM, and developing awareness among residents regarding the purpose of the new city plan. The Satoumi Promotion Section was then established in the city government as the coordinating mechanism for ICM, and the Shima City Satoumi Creation Basic Plan (Shima City ICM Basic Plan) became a high priority project from 2011 to 2015. The Shima City Satoumi Creation Basic Plan (Shima City ICM Basic Plan) was drafted with the participation of a wide variety of stakeholder groups. The Basic Plan lists guidelines for measures aimed at the sustainable use of natural resources and is centred around the philosophy of satoumi. In 1998, Tetsuo Yanagi, an oceanographer at Kyushu University, defined this as coastal landscapes where humans play a beneficial role in the sustainability and health of the ocean: satoumi is a combination of the words for villages (sato) and the sea (umi). After the success of the first plan, a new Basic Plan was implemented in March 2016, to cover the five-year period between 2016 and 2020 (Matsuda et al., 2019; Uranaka, 2012, 2017, 2018) (Figure 7.3).

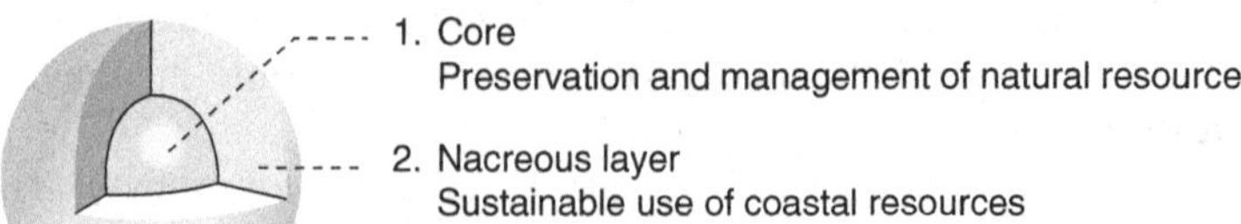

Figure 7.3 Shima City's coastal management approach, depicted through the properties of a pearl.

7.3 Tidal flat restoration projects

Population decline was also seen as an opportunity to make a difference. The smaller number of pearl cultivators at sea reduced the burden on the marine environment. At the same time, the city identified many small areas of former rice paddy by the sea that had been abandoned, due to the aging demographic of farmers and lifestyle changes. The common practice of land reclamation in small inlets by citizens seems to have started around the 1700s (Ago Town, 2000; Daio Town, 1994; Hamashima Town, 1989; Shima Town, 2004). In the twentieth century, when there were food shortages during and after the wars, the government told citizens that where they put a sea dike across a small inlet and drained the water, any reclaimed land would be theirs. Many people took this opportunity to turn the tidal flats into rice fields. Local people used these lands until rice became cheaper and modern lifestyles made managing them more difficult, as they were often hard to reach from the residential areas on the hill or were accessible only by boat.

To solve the unhealthy level of nutrients in Ago Bay, the municipal government tried to encourage citizens to carry out domestic wastewater management, as well as participate in dredging activities in the bay (Uranaka, 2018). At the same time, the project team realised that many small plots of land by the shore had been abandoned, and water flow from the mountains to the sea had also been blocked by the dikes on this land. By restoring the links between forests and the sea, the nutrient circulation mechanisms would be restored, and the revived tidal flats would host many living creatures. We also remembered that during the mid-1950s Tadao Sato, a scientist and pioneer of Japanese oyster culture, opposed the idea of water desalination in the inner part of Matoya Bay for agricultural use. He persuaded people by saying that cutting the flow of nutrition from the mountains to the ocean would damage the fisheries of Matoya Bay. As a result, the plan was withdrawn.

With the cooperation of the Shima municipal government, Mie prefectural government, Mie Fishery Research Centre, OPRI and fishers, tidal flat restoration project ideas started to emerge among a small number of groups. The scientific evidence for the benefits of these restorations will be discussed in Chapter 8. In the past, creating land from the tidal flats for rice harvests was regarded as forward-thinking city planning, yet now, recreating tidal flats on unused rice paddies is seen as progressive. The initiative to convert abandoned shorelines into tidal flats received the 2014 Hitachi Environment Foundation and the Nikkan Kogyo Shimbun Environmental Award in recognition of its achievement in conserving the environment through coordinating activities of local stakeholders at little expense. These activities also received the Prime Minister's Award for the Ocean Nation Promotion Merit in 2015. In 2016, Shima City's Kashikojima Island hosted the G7 Ise-Shima Summit due to its successful preservation of some of Japan's most beautiful natural environments and traditional culture.

7.4 Learning from promoting tidal flat restoration projects

In this section, I would like to share three main things I have learnt from the experience of promoting tidal flat restorations, especially around participation, coordination and resources.

7.4.1 Encouraging residents' participation

The researchers involved in the restoration projects put much time and effort into making sure their explanations about the tidal restoration projects were clear and conducted various events to bring residents closer to the tidal flat restoration activities. These researchers, including Hideki Kokubu who writes the next chapter, understood the importance of working with citizens. Making links between residents and the restoration ideas brought new opportunities from one restoration to the next. We, the local government officers, therefore focused our efforts on making links with outside researchers and local stakeholders, and hosted events to inform people about the projects' outcomes.

Originally, when we tried to explain the restoration project ideas to residents, they did not seem too certain about the benefits. This might be because many people rarely have the chance to get to know or go to tidal flats nowadays. To respond to this situation, we conducted educational programmes for young people to experience the tidal flats and see the kinds of things they nurture including aosa seaweed, which a delicacy of Shima city.

The fourth tidal flat restoration site received the backing of the local councils. The restoration work required at that site was mainly removing sandbags from across the small water channel, so the volunteers simply got into the shallow area of the sea and removed them individually by hand. In Shima, there are still many possible sites to be restored, and the challenge is to encourage citizens themselves to become even more motivated to restore this land and engage administrative and governmental officials to make it happen.

7.4.2 Coordinating across different agencies and landowners

Whenever we conducted tidal flat restoration projects, we needed to obtain approval not only from the landowners to return their land to tidal flats, but also from the people who own the surrounding land. The restoration activities in Ago Bay introduce seawater onto wetlands or dry land, and there is a risk that the surrounding land will receive salt damage due to the activity. Therefore, the governmental offices decided that in order to conduct such activities in Ago Bay, written approval must be obtained from all the landowners, including those of the surrounding land. To identify all the landowners, we needed information from the Legal Affairs Bureau, and got in touch with them.

Also, within the different governmental organisations, the Shima Municipal Office together with the Mie Prefecture Fisheries Research Institute needed to explain our project to the Agricultural Infrastructure Section of the Mie Prefectural Office, which is responsible for the water gates of the sea dikes of the reclaimed land. They could not allow water gates to be opened unless they obtained approval from the surrounding landowners too. These approval procedures were new and initially difficult to achieve, but the more we conducted tidal flat restoration projects, the more understanding spread among the Agricultural Infrastructure Section members. We succeeded in developing shared rules and procedures for tidal flat restorations.

Difficulties arose when the owners of potential land for restoration had died and the inheritance process was incomplete. The Ago Bay tidal flat restoration projects currently have a premise that restoration activities are conducted on reclaimed land that is no longer in use. When such land has not been officially passed on to a family member, current Japanese law automatically passes ownership to all the deceased's siblings, who then have rights to use or sell the land. In such circumstances, approval must be obtained from all the heirs to conduct tidal flat restorations; however, it is often very difficult to find them. With an ageing population, having multiple owners of a small piece of land will only increase, making the restoration process extremely complicated. Nationally, we need to come up with new ideas and legislation on how to look after and utilise abandoned land, which is increasingly prevalent in the community.

7.4.3 Issues of financial resources

It is still difficult to decide who pays the cost of restoration activities when funding is required, such as the administration cost. So far, the administrative costs incurred in supporting the inheritance process and changes in land registration (e.g. from farmland to mixed land). Also, in the future, a project might need to purchase land which needs civil engineering work, such as drainage, so that seawater can be introduced onto the land in a controlled way when the water gate is opened.

So far, we have chosen sites that need little funding to conduct the restoration activities. However, it will become increasingly important to consider ways to cover the costs surrounding them. They could include not only the conventional use of taxpayers' money from local government, but also other methods such as crowd funding, or a sponsoring mechanism which provides some kind of benefit or experience to citizens who donate.

7.5 Conclusion

People in Shima City traditionally lived by utilising the bounty from the forests and the sea. Henceforth, these coastal regions will be utilised not only through the agricultural and fishing industries, but also tourism and human resource development to revitalise the local area. We will look at the environment as a whole, not only discussing the prevention of ocean pollution, but also the importance of tidal flats and seagrass bed restoration projects and abandoned forest management. Our goal is developing a blue economy, which is firmly rooted in local people's lives, and to sustainably utilise the coastal environment to match the needs of society.

Ise-Shima National Park represents the Japanese National Park management style, striving for humans to be a part of nature, linking the rich environment with societal and economical activities for sustainable societies (satoyama and satoumi). This is a different style of management compared to traditional European or US models which try to keep nature untouched.

To promote these types of conservation efforts, the term 'satoumi' was easily accepted by the Japanese audience; however, in the future, it will be necessary for us to also use different terms to tackle environmental conservation activities which are recognised by people all over the world. Considering the coastal environment is very much under the influence of global environmental change, this is extremely important. We often say 'think global, act local', and in acting local, it is helpful to use the Sustainable Development Goals and targets to liaise and link with people who are trying to solve the same issues across the world.

Tidal flat restorations are important activities to build a rich ocean biodiversity, which supports us in building a blue economy. To raise these restoration activities to another level, we should not restrict ourselves to the current ways of working, such as depending solely on the understanding and goodwill of landowners and only conducting projects with little cost attached. I think we could potentially develop tidal flat restoration projects by operating these activities alongside other organisations such as the National Trust, with public funding attached for nature conservation.

7.6 Implication for future practice and research needs

In terms of the ladder of participation for citizens, Ago Bay tidal flat restoration projects showed how the local government started with incremental steps to start 'authorities-initiated, shared decisions with citizens' at the early stages of the restoration project. They provided plenty of scientific data, assurances about the precautionary principal (e.g. letters confirming that if individuals suffer negative effects on their land due to the project they will receive compensation), and visits to individuals to make sure the worries which landowners have can be addressed before starting the projects. There were many other lessons from this case study.

7.6.1 Implication for future practice

I learnt two things from my experience of the Ago Bay tidal flat restoration projects:

- High motivation among the people involved in a project is the key to keeping it on track to obtain results. This project recruited volunteers from among researchers who wanted to get involved with the project as well as from staff from the newly created governmental Satoumi Promotion Office (later known as SDGs Future City Promotion Office), which coordinates all the sustainable ocean related activities in the municipal office. This way of creating the team across specialisms worked well to maintain motivation.
- It is vital to work with local people and not merely present them with a report at the end of the project. During the research work, the research team involved local people in various ways and held feedback meetings very frequently. The fact that the researchers worked closely with the stakeholders throughout the project made it easier to feed back the outcomes of the project directly to the community and those involved.

7.6.2 Future research needs

- After the Ago Bay Project ended, we had to scale down the ocean monitoring system due to reduced research funding. In the face of global climate change, monitoring data is essential in understanding what is happening in our oceans, such as why huge numbers of pearl shells died suddenly in 2020.
- The more essential environmental monitoring becomes, the more our need for quantitative methods to understand ecosystem changes gets stronger. Currently in Ago Bay, we are continuing research activities on tidal flat living creatures with the help of citizens, and the results show changes in the dominant species and their numbers year on year. I feel it is important to build ecosystem monitoring systems in the future that include not only researchers but also stakeholders.

References

Ago Town (2000) *Ago cho shi* [The history of Ago Town]. Shima City: Ago Town.

Daio Town (1994) *Dao cho shi* [The history of Daio Town]. Shima City: Daio Town.

Hamashima Town (1989) *Hamashima cho shi* [The history of Hamashima Town]. Shima City: Hamashima Town.

Matsuda, O., Kokubu, H. and Uranaka, H. (2019) 'Agowan saisei project no sokatsu to sonogo no tenkai' [Summary of the Ago Bay restoration projects and the future development]. *Nippon suisan gakkai* [Japan Fishery Association], 75(4), 737–742.

Shima Town (2004) *Shima cho shi* [The history of Shima Town]. Shima City: Shima Town.

Statistics Bureau of Japan (2015) *Population Census*. Tokyo: Statistics Bureau of Japan.

Uranaka, H. (2012) Atarashii satoumi no machi Shima o mezashite [Aiming for a new satoumi city, Shima] *Kokuritsu Koen* [National Parks], Vol. 703, May 2012. Tokyo: Shizen Koen Zaidan [Nature Park Foundation], pp.2–6.

Uranaka, H. (2017) 'Atarashii satoumi no machi Shimashi no higata saisei' [Tidal flat restorations in new satoumi Shima City]. *Mizu kankyo gakkai shi* [Journal of Japan Society on Water Environment], 40(11), 398–401.

Uranaka, H. (2018) 'Shima shi no higata saisei' [Tidal flat restoration in Shima City]. *Presentation material, International Tidal Flat Restoration Symposium*. Shima City, Japan, 19 May 2018.

8 Creating the first tidal flat restoration project in Japan in Ago Bay

Hideki Kokubu

8.1 Introduction

After the 1960s, Japanese policies towards environmental conservation and management concentrated on water pollution control mainly by reducing terrestrial pollutants. However, this kind of passive conservation policy, which strengthened pollution controls, is gradually shifting towards active conservation. 'Satoumi' promotes the restoration of biodiversity, biological productivity, habitats and a well-balanced nutrient cycle between the land and the sea (Secretariat of the Convention on Biological Diversity, 2011; Berque and Matsuda, 2013). Holistic approaches such as ecosystem-based management and integrated coastal management (ICM) are also being incorporated in new policies; the former promoting the restoration of biodiversity, and the latter the interaction between land and sea.

In response to the negative environmental changes and their effect on local fisheries and communities, scientists, central and local government, the private sector and residents jointly organised the Ago Bay Restoration Project, based on the new concept of satoumi, from 2003 to 2007 (Yanagi, 2007; Matsuda, 2010; Matsuda and Kokubu, 2011). The authors of Chapters 7 and 8 both joined the project.

More than a century ago, many tidal flats existed in the inner part of the bay. However, between the 1850s and 1940s their numbers drastically decreased, as many dikes were constructed in order to prevent the intrusion of seawater onto expanded rice fields (Ago Town, 2000). In 2005 and 2010, the status of tidal flats and reclaimed areas was investigated through visual observation, listening to residents and bibliographic surveys.

From scientific research on this project, it was clear that approximately 70% of tidal flat areas had been lost through land development,

DOI: 10.4324/9780367863098-8

Figure 8.1 An educational activity on one of the restored tidal flats.

namely dike construction and land reclamation, which interfered with the natural connectivity between the land and coastal seas. Dike construction blocked the tidal exchange, creating a hypertrophic wetland of fresh or brackish water on the inner side of the dikes. The distribution of the reclaimed areas around Ago bay in 2010 is shown in Figure 8.2.

The utilisation status of reclaimed areas and their characteristic appearance in 2005 and 2010 are shown in Table 8.1. There were 0.84 km^2 of existing tidal flats in 2005, with 0.03 km^2 of estuarine tidal flats and 0.81 km^2 of foreshore tidal flats. Reclaimed areas covered 1.76 km^2, of which 41 sites (0.31 km^2) were still cultivating paddies in 2005. In 2010, paddy fields decreased to 19 sites (0.23 km^2); uncultivated areas included 463 sites (1.45 km^2) in 2005 and 485 sites (1.53 km^2) in 2010. Of these, about 25% were used for other purposes in 2005 and 2010. Most of these uncultivated areas were small (under 0.01 km^2). About 58% of the dikes were made using bonded stone, and about 23% of them had problems with seawater flowing into the uncultivated areas. Ten dikes had collapsed.

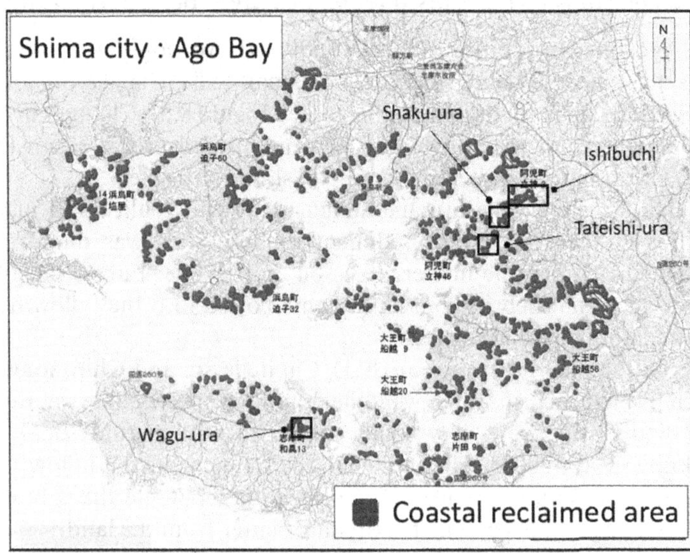

Figure 8.2 Distribution of the reclaimed areas around Ago Bay in 2010 (Mie prefecture).

Table 8.1 The utilisation status of reclaimed areas and their characteristic appearance in 2005 and 2010

Monitoring period			*Number*	*Area (ha)*
Natural tidal flat	2005	Estuarine	-	3.0
		Foreshore	-	81.0
Cultivation satate	2005	Fallow field	463	145.3
		Cultivated field	41	31.0
	2010	Fallow field	485	153.3
		Cultivated field	19	23.0
Utilisation situation of follow fields	2005	Wetland, Wasteland	-	108.9
		Used, Other	-	36.4
	2010	Wetland, Wasteland	378	115.2
		Used, Other	107	38.1
Shape of dike	2010	Concrete	210	-
		Stone bond	294	-
State of floodgate	2010	Collapsed	10	-
		Seawater intrusion	117	-
		Workable	387	-
State of reclaimed area	2010	1ha<	33	-
		1ha>	471	-

8.2 Conditions of the unused reclaimed areas before restoration

The Ago Bay Restoration Project conducted two tidal flat restoration trials to collect baseline measures: a small-scale trial at Shaku-ura followed by the main trial at Ishibuchi (see Figure 8.3). Changes in sediment quality and macro-benthos were monitored every season for a year. The monitoring sites and dates are shown in Table 8.2.

Table 8.2 shows the average annual sediment quality and macro-benthos at these sites. The sediment in both sites was muddy and contained rich organic matter (Kokubu et al., 2008; Furota, 2000). It is presumed that debris from land plants flowed into the fallow fields, accumulating behind the dikes.

From the macro-benthos analysis, Capitella sp. and Chironomidae, which live in brackish water, were the dominant species. The wet weight and biodiversity were very small compared with natural tidal flats (Kokubu et al., 2008). The sediment environment in the fallow fields became eutrophic and anaerobic because the concrete dikes blocked tidal exchange and accumulated organic matter from the land.

Table 8.2 Annual characteristics of sediment quality (DL+0.5m) and macro-benthos in the trial sites before tidal exchange in Ago Bay

			Unused reclaimed area (behind dikes)	
			Syaku-ura	*Ishibuchi*
	Sampling date		*Feb.'06, Jun. '06 Sep. '06, Jan. '07*	*May '05, Jul. '05 Oct. '05, Jan. '05*
	Sampling depth (DL)		*+1.0m, + 0.5m, 0m*	*+1.0m, + 0.5m, 0m*
Sediment quality (DL + 0.5m)	Appearance		Muddy	Muddy
	Mud content	(%)	78.6 ± 5.4	75.1 ± 5.7
	COD	($mg^{+}g^{-1}$ $-dry^{-1}$)	86.1 ± 5.3	74.2 ± 4.6
	TOC	($mg+g^{-1}$ $-dry^{-1}$)	56.7 ± 1.5	43.5 ± 2.4
	TN	($mg^{+}g^{-1}$ $-dry^{-1}$)	4.6 ± .0.2	3.8 ± 1.9
	AVS	($mg^{+}g^{-1}$ $-dry^{-1}$)	4.7 ± 2.1	2.9 ± 0.2
	C/N ratio		12.5 ± 1.5	12.7 ± 0.4
Macro benthos	Density	(ind. $^{+}0.2m^{-2}$)	109.4 ± 17.2	176.2 ± 32.8
	Species	(species $^{+}0.2m^{-2}$)	7.1 ± 0.8	13.0 ± 1.4
	Wet weight	($g^{+}0.2m^{-2}$)	3.6 ± 1.2	5.4 ± 1.3
	Wet weight (Ave)	($g^{+}ind.^{-1}$)	0.04 ± 0.01	0.05 ± 0.02

• Present (Decrease in the land-ocean interaction)

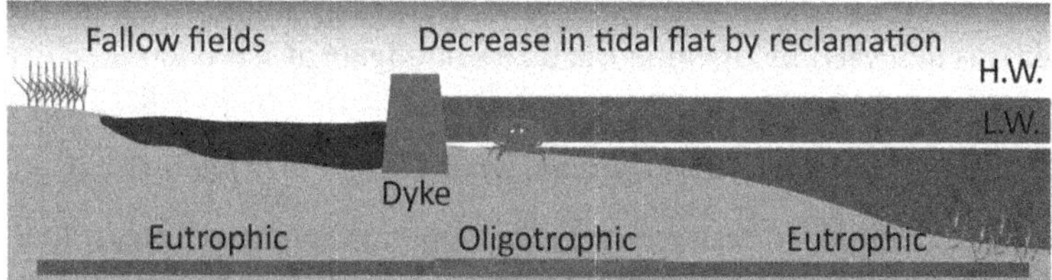

• After promoting tidal exchange (Restore the land-ocean interaction)

1. Promoting tidal exchangeby using pump (Feasibility experiment)

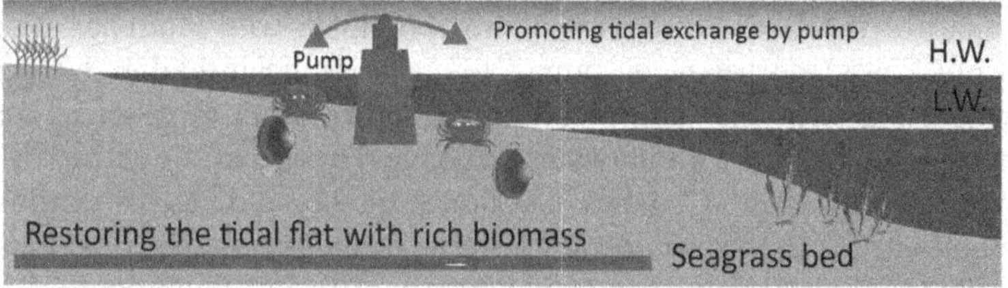

2. Promoting tidal exchange by opening the floodgate

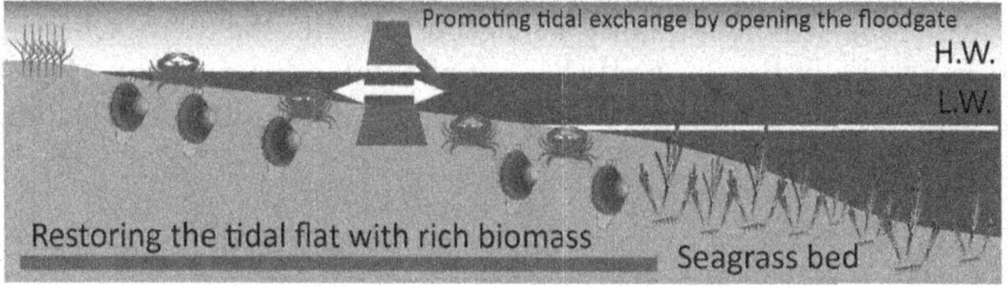

Figure 8.3 Conceptual illustration of the trial design of tidal flat restoration. Key: H.W.: high water; L.W.: low water.

The sediment of unused wetlands has a high organic matter content because the dikes cause an accumulation of nutrient run-off from the land. In these areas, the abundance and diversity of macro-benthos is quite poor (Figure 8.3).

8.3 The Ago Bay Restoration Project trials

Two sites of unused wetland in Ago Bay were selected as trial sites where existing dikes divided reclaimed wetland areas (inside the dikes) and natural tidal flats (outside the dikes). The natural tidal water exchange across the dikes had been blocked at both trial sites, preventing seawater intrusion and fresh water accumulating inside could only leave through the floodgate. In this study, promotion of water exchange across the dikes was carried out using two different methods. One was the promotion of water exchange through water pumps at Shaku-ura, and the other was achieved by opening the dike's floodgate at Ishibuchi.

8.3.1 Small-scale tidal flat restoration trial: Using water pumps

A small-scale tidal flat restoration trial using water pumps to create artificial tidal exchange was conducted from 2006 to 2010 at Shaku-ura (see Figure 8.4). A concrete dike had blocked tidal exchange between both sides, with the inner side being used to cultivate rice. In the experiment, this part of the dike was separated into two blocks with sandbags. The test block used electric water pumps to create artificial tidal exchange, harmonising with the natural tides. The other block was set as an experimental control without water exchange. The size of the entire trial site was about 400 m^2. Changes in sediment quality and macro-benthos were monitored in the test and control blocks and the natural tidal flats outside the dike every season from 2006 to 2010. Sampling points are shown in Figure 8.4.

Changes in sediment quality were observed after the tidal exchange. Figure 8.5 shows the seasonal changes of total organic carbon (TOC) and acid volatile sulphide (AVS) at a height of +0.5 m (DL=Datum

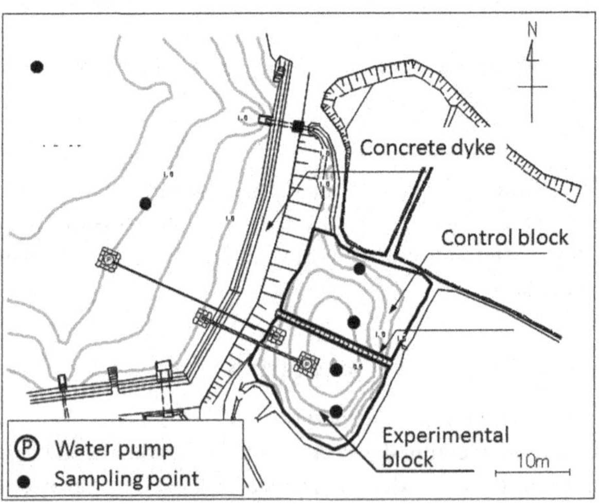

Figure 8.4 Outline of the same-scale trial site (Shaku-ura).

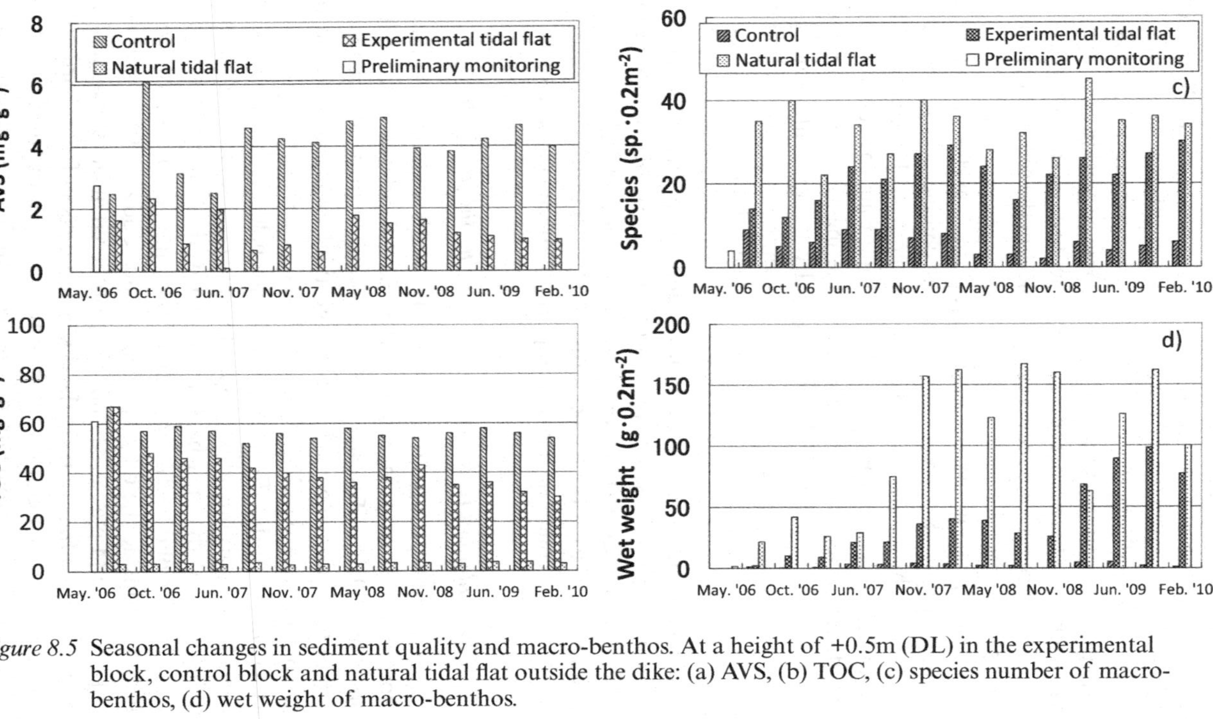

Figure 8.5 Seasonal changes in sediment quality and macro-benthos. At a height of +0.5m (DL) in the experimental block, control block and natural tidal flat outside the dike: (a) AVS, (b) TOC, (c) species number of macro-benthos, (d) wet weight of macro-benthos.

Line) in the test block, control block and natural tidal flats in front of the dike. Before the experiment, both TOC and AVS in the test block were high and anaerobic. TOC and AVS in the test block gradually decreased and were significantly lower than in the control block 18 months later. These results indicate that the sediment environment in the test block gradually changed from anaerobic to aerobic conditions by promoting tidal exchange between the sea and the test block. Therefore, the organic compounds and reducing substances in the sediment apparently decreased.

Positive change in macro-benthos after water exchange also became apparent. Figure 8.5 shows the seasonal change of species number and wet weight of the macro-benthos in the test block, control block and natural tidal flats. Before the trial, only four species were found. Immediately after the water exchange, the macro-benthos in the test block changed from brackish species to saltwater and eutrophic species. Eighteen months later, 29 types of macro-benthos were found in the test block, such as bivalves and crustaceans. The volume of macro-benthos in the control block stayed at a low level. As previously indicated, the organic compounds in the test block sediment decomposed. Therefore, it is assumed that the sediment environment gradually changed to suitable conditions for the macro-benthos (Kuwae, 2005; Japan Fisheries Resource Conservation Association, 2000). These results suggest that land–ocean interactions are very important around coastal areas.

8.3.2 Main tidal flat restoration trial: Opening the floodgate

Based on these positive results from the small-scale trial, a tidal flat restoration trial involving opening the dike's floodgate was conducted from April 2010 to February 2012 at Ishibuchi in Ago Bay. Opening the floodgate was expected to promote tidal exchange between both sides of the dike (see Figure 8.6). This approximately 20,000 m^2 site was reclaimed in the 1960s to cultivate rice fields. However, more than 20 years ago, rice cultivation stopped due to changes in socio-economic conditions, and the area became unused wetland inside the seawater-intrusion control dike. In this trial, tidal exchange was introduced onto the wetland inside the dike by opening the floodgate. Changes in sediment quality and macro-benthos were observed at the site as well as at the natural tidal flats outside the dike every season from April 2010 to February 2012. The sampling points are shown in Figure 8.6.

As well as improvements in sediment quality and macro-benthos, positive changes in sediment quality after tidal exchange were also observed. Figure 8.7 shows the seasonal changes of AVS, chemical

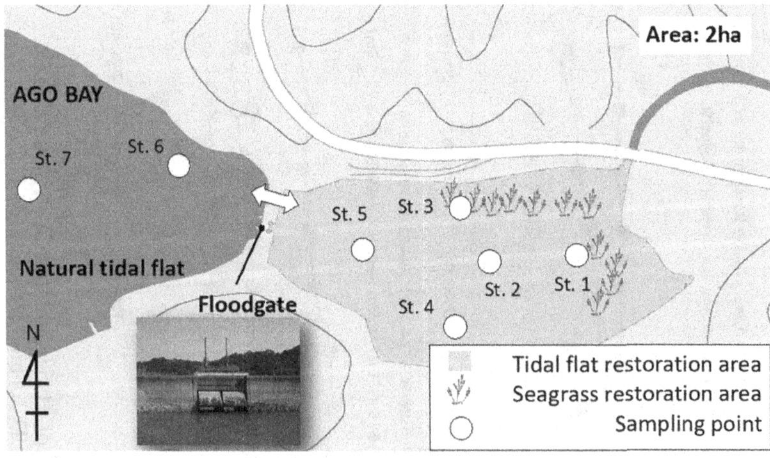

Figure 8.6 The trial site (Ishibuchi) promoting tidal exchange by opening the floodgate.

oxygen demand (COD), mud content and TOC at a height of +0.5 m and 0 m (St. 3, 5, 6, 7) at the restoration site and natural tidal flats in front of the dike. Before tidal exchange, the sediment at the restoration site was muddy and anaerobic. AVS, COD, mud content and TOC at the restoration site were all significantly high compared with those of the natural tidal flats. Immediately after tidal exchange, AVS at the restoration site decreased from 2.8 to 0.6 mg/g. Three months later, COD, mud content and TOC also started to decrease gradually, especially in shallower areas (St. 3). However, in the natural tidal flats outside the dike, the sediment quality did not change as obviously. These results are the same as in the feasibility trial shown above. It is assumed that the sediment environment at the restoration site gradually changed from anaerobic to aerobic conditions through tidal exchange between the sea and the restoration site. Therefore, organic compounds and reducing substances in the sediment probably decreased.

Positive changes of macro-benthos occurred after water exchange. Figure 8.8 shows the seasonal change in the species number and the wet weight of macro-benthos at a height of +0.5 m and 0 m (St. 3, 5, 6, 7) at the restoration site and natural tidal flats in front of the dike. Figure 8.8 shows changes in the number of macro-benthos, classified as insects, crustaceans, gastropoda, bivalves and polychaeta at a height of +0.5 m at the restoration site and natural tidal flats (St. 3 and 6).

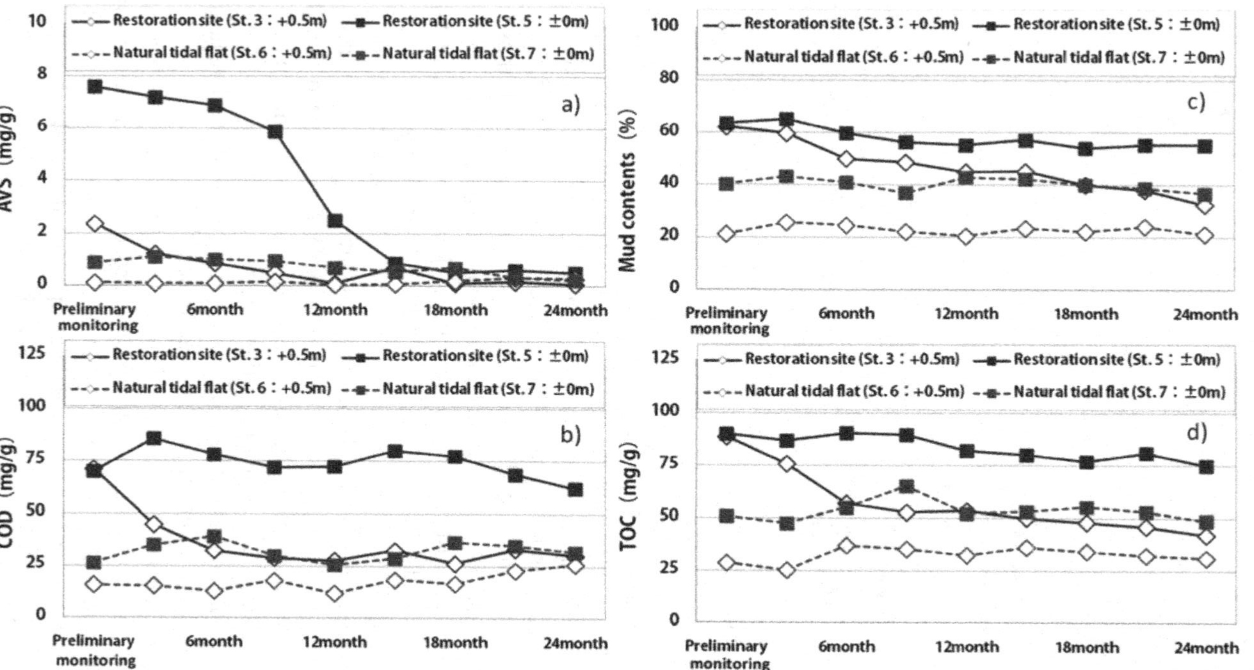

Figure 8.7 Seasonal changes of AVS, COD, mud contents and TOC. At a height of +0.5 m and 0 m (St. 3, 5, 6, 7) in the restoration site and natural tidal flats outside the dike: (a) AVS, (b) COD, (c) mud contents, (d) TOC.

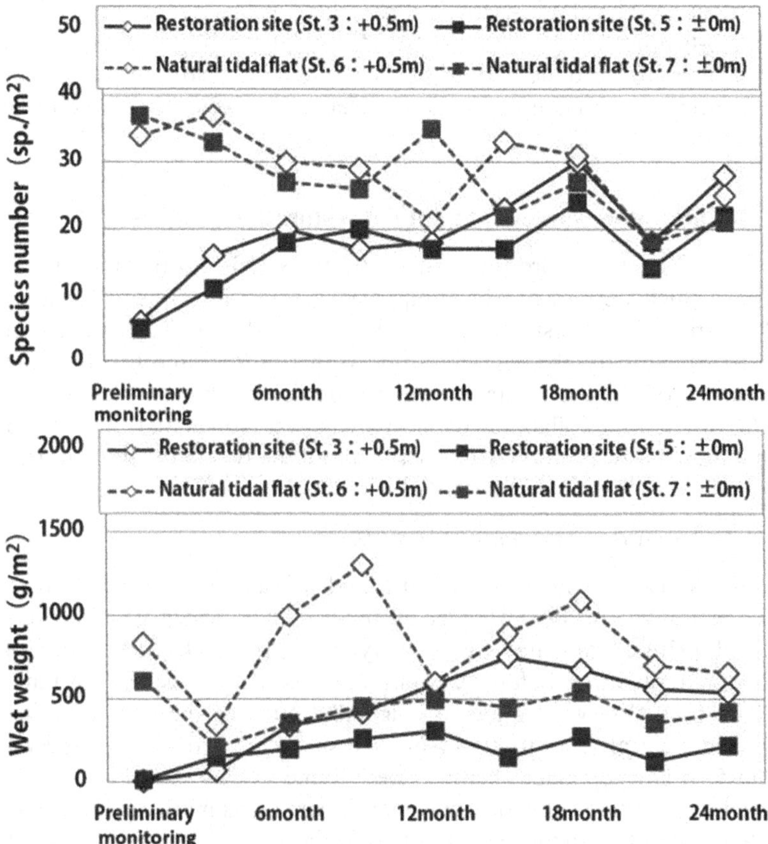

Figure 8.8 Seasonal change in species number and wet weight of macro-benthos. At a height of +0.5 m and 0 m (St. 3, 5, 6, 7) in the restoration site and natural tidal flats outside the dike.

Immediately after tidal exchange, the salinity at the restoration site increased from 15 to 32. Before tidal exchange, only six species living in brackish and eutrophic areas, such as Capitella sp. and Chironomidae, were found at the restoration site. Three months later, insects disappeared and polychaeta, such as Hediste sp., increased. Twelve months later, fixable types of macro-benthos, such as *Musculus senhousia* and *Ruditapes philippinarum*, increased. The wet weight of the macro-benthos at the restoration site (St. 3) gradually increased from 7.2 to 750 g from 24 months. Many juvenile fish, such as *Mugil cephalus*, *Lateolabrax japonicus* and *Acanthogobius flavimanus* were also found at the restoration site by visual investigation. From these results it is confirmed that macro-benthos gradually increased after tidal exchange. It is expected that biological productivity in the coastal fallow fields will be further enhanced through continuing tidal exchange between the sea and these fields.

8.4 Three more successful tidal flat restoration projects

In Ago Bay, two more tidal flat restorations (Niu-no-Ike and Otani-Ura), which were owned by companies involved in tourism, began in 2012 and another restoration, which was owned by citizens, started in 2016. Shima City, the Mie Prefecture Fisheries Research Institute, the Ministry of the Environment, the private companies and the citizens who own the site collaborated and shared a common goal. It is expected that tidal flat restoration will spread around the Bay in the near future.

8.4.1 Restoration case study: Niu-no-Ike

This restoration was started in 2012 and was a collaboration between Nemu Resort (previously called Nemu-no-Sato), which is a tourism-based private company, Shima City and Mie Prefecture Fisheries Research Institute. Before restoration, unused areas were eutrophic, and biodiversity was as low as originally found at the Ishibuchi site. Immediately after restoration, biodiversity increased. Twelve species and 53.6 g/m^2 of macro-benthos were found at this site in 2013. The hotel began using the restoration site as part of its marketing strategy, offering nature tours for visitors. The ocean side of the sea dike is used by local fishers as an aquaculture site for aosa seaweed. The nutrients from the forest now pass directly to the sea, enhancing seaweed growth.

8.4.2 Restoration case study: Otani-ura

This restoration was a collaboration between Miyako Resort Okushima Aqua Forest Aqua Villa Hotel (previously called Hotel Kintstsu Aqua Villa Ise-Shima), which is tourism-based private company, and the Ministry of the Environment and Shima City, and started in 2012. This was conducted under the Appropriate Oceanic Management Promotion Project for the National Park (so-called 'marine worker project'). The restoration was mainly managed by the Ministry of Environment as a symbol of Ise-Shima National Park. Before restoration, unused areas were eutrophic and biodiversity was very low, as in the Ishibuchi site.

Immediately after opening the floodgate, the once poor oxygen levels of the area improved dramatically and an increase in biodiversity was identified. Unique to this site, the seagrass bed (*Zostera japonica*) increased approximately five times in size compared to the pre-restoration period. No negative impact to the ocean in front of the floodgate was observed.

8.4.3 Restoration case study: Wagu-ura

This restoration was the first case where the site owners were private citizens. It was a collaboration between the residents' association and Shima City and began in 2016. The restoration was negotiated between the residents' association and the site owner. This site already had some water exchange between the sea and the reclaimed area because part of the dike was damaged. Then Shima City and the volunteers promoted more water exchange by removing the sandbags used as dikes. After the restoration, more than 30 species of macro-benthos were found. Near to this site, there are primary and junior high schools, a fisheries high school and the fisheries research laboratory of Mie University. It is expected that this site is going to be used for environmental education.

8.5 Building win–win relationships with other governmental departments and the public

What I always had in mind was to build win–win relationships among those who are involved in this project, and to communicate the effects of tidal flat restorations to the public as clearly as possible. I would like to share some thoughts here.

8.5.1 Involving the municipal government in tidal flat restoration

The Shima City government has been actively engaged in satoumi-oriented coastal environment restoration since 2010, and tidal flat restoration has been incorporated into the city's official new planning policy, which covers most aspects of Ago Bay management. As stated earlier, the Basic Plan of Satoumi Creation established by the Shima City government is also authorised as a Basic ICM Plan of the area.

The long-term commitment of scientists to the local community, in cooperation with the administrative staff of the city office, many local volunteers and NGOs has been essential in the satoumi activities for restoration. It is hoped that their efforts will continue to support the area's conservation projects and encourage sustainable use of the marine environment within the satoumi framework. This has now developed into a Shima ESDs Future City project to further expand their work across the city.

8.5.2 Communication and mandate barriers among different governmental sections

As mentioned above, there are 485 such reclaimed areas in Ago Bay, totalling as much as 1.53 km^2; once developed, but now just unused fields such as wetlands. The results of this study indicate that to enhance biological productivity around coastal areas, it is necessary to promote tidal flat restoration. However, this is problematic due to poor communication among each governmental division. In Japan, the coastline is managed mainly by the Ministry of Land, Infrastructure, Transport, and Tourism. Ago Bay itself is designated as a National Park and is therefore under the jurisdiction of the Ministry of the Environment; the dikes themselves are managed mainly by the Ministry of Agriculture, Forestry and Fisheries, as part of their agriculture operations. Most of the unused fields are owned by individuals or businesses. The challenge is to convince these owners that their land is recoverable and could be profitable after restoration.

Another challenge is to achieve collaboration between the municipal, prefectural and national governments. Table 8.3 shows how different areas in the city are managed by separate governmental departments and mandates. I often visited these departments even when I did not have anything in particular to discuss, just to stay in contact. Getting to know people and their mandate barriers was very time-consuming, yet most rewarding. These informal chats built trust allowing us to create ways around the existing national rules and develop local strategies, gaining experience over time.

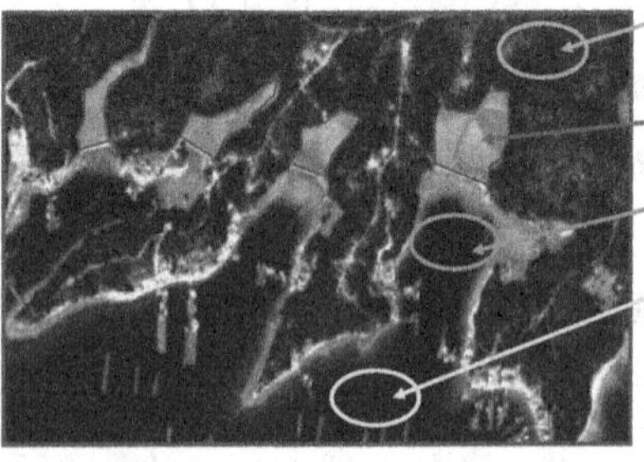

Figure 8.9 Complex governing structure around the coastal area in Japan.

Table 8.3 How different areas in the city are managed by separate governmental departments and mandates

Areas in the city	*Governmental department responsible for management*	*Mandate*
National Park	Ministry of Environment	To protect and control development in the National Park
Unused fields	Ministry of Agriculture, Forestry and Fisheries (prefecture and city)	To protect and control development in the agricultural fields
Coastal area	Ministry of Land, Infrastructure and Transport (prefecture and city)	To protect against disasters and control development in coastal area
Sea area	Prefectural Fishery Section	To protect the sea environment and control fishery catches

8.5.3 Building up public enthusiasm

I tried to create mechanisms whereby those involved in the project could join in activities and experience the direct benefits of the restorations. For example, we conducted research activities with the participants, releasing juvenile asari clams and planting seaweed, and cultivating aosa seaweed. Six months later we held another event to check the effects of the activities and collected seafood to eat together. I saw how this deepened the citizens' understanding of the restoration activities they had participated in and how greatly they had enjoyed them.

In terms of building win–win relationships, I listened to all the individuals who were associated with this project to understand the obstacles in them getting involved in the restoration. We then created a system whereby those from different offices within the government and from different sectors could feel some benefit from being a part of this project.

To promote understanding and local involvement, activities such as monthly observation tours and seaweed planting by volunteers were conducted at the restoration sites. Other plans are to plant seed clams and to cultivate green seaweed on site, to be harvested later. In addition, the cooperation of the media was important. Many people came to know about the project through newspapers and the TV, and that in turn prompted other media to become interested in our work, helping us to widen our activities.

8.6 Conclusion: Future tidal flat restoration in Japan

The major findings of this study are summarised as follows: (1) land reclamation and construction of dikes interfered with the habitats of macro-benthos and the material circulation between land and coastal seas; (2) after promoting tidal exchange, the sediment conditions at the restoration sites gradually changed to aerobic conditions and organic compounds, and reducing substances gradually decreased; (3) this induced an increase in both the number of species and wet weight of macro-benthos. These results suggest that improvement of the sediment environment and enhancement of biological productivity can be expected to occur when restoring unused coastal wetlands to more natural tidal flats.

Ago Bay has achieved four tidal flat restoration projects. Originally, it was started only by a small group of local aquaculture fishers and researchers, but this led to establishing links with the Shima municipal office and Ministry of Environment. Then local companies endorsed these activities by opening up water gates to utilise their unused land and ponds as corporate social responsibility activities. In 2016, with the approval of local council members, restoration activity was conducted on unused coastal land owned by residents. Slowly, restoration activities are spreading across the community.

In Japan, more than 30,000 ha of tidal flats were reclaimed after soaring economic growth from the mid-1950s through to the 1960s (Nature Conservation Bureau, 1994). Sohma et al. (2008) reported that the reclamation of tidal flats has a fatal impact on coastal ecosystems, causing red tides, hypoxia, the death of macro-benthos etc. There are many unused reclaimed areas around urban coastal zones, such as Tokyo Bay and Ise Bay. More than 60,000 ha of the unused areas exist near coastal zones (Ministry of Land, Infrastructure, Transport and Tourism, 2002).

In order to enhance the biological productivity and diversity of unused coastal wetlands, tidal flat restoration trials were conducted by promoting tidal exchange between the sea and coastal wetlands across dikes in Ago Bay; the effects were very clear.

We have no desire to decry past land reclamation activities. It must have been necessary to reclaim areas of inlets to increase food production to support the citizens at that time. However, the social situation has changed dramatically since then, and it is necessary to have the courage to choose an adaptive policy, which fits the current situation. Tidal flat restoration is one option to utilise unused coastal land. I strongly hope that we can expand this activity to the 485 similar environments in the area in the future. To achieve this would require open debate and cooperation between local citizens and governmental offices, utilising an integrated coastal management philosophy. Without this, we cannot have true satoumi and restoration in Ago Bay. We can only take small steps, but we are willing to tackle this huge task one step at a time.

8.7 Implication for future practice and research needs

8.7.1 Implication for future practice

- Present clear, scientific explanations about the project by researching the causes of the current issues and potential restoration effects.
- Identify all the stakeholders in a tidal flat restoration, foster mutual understanding and build win–win relationships wherever possible.
- Secure funding but prepare strategies to try and prevent activities ending if funding ceases or personnel leave (this is something we have not achieved yet).
- Never give up (the Ago Bay restoration project was 10 years in the planning).
- Conduct public relations (PR) activities by utilising the media, social media, environmental education and company commercials to let many people know about the project.
- Clearly explain the benefits and effectiveness of nature restoration to all local citizens indirectly involved in the project.
- Plan fun events alongside restoration activities – without engagement, the activities will not last.

8.7.2 Future research needs

- Visualisation of the effectiveness of tidal flat restorations, via simulations or other means.
- Identification of the social and legal systems needed to conduct local consensus building.

References

Ago Town (2000) *Ago cho shi* [The history of Ago Town]. Shima City: Ago Town.

Berque, J. and Matsuda, O. (2013) 'Coastal biodiversity management in Japanese satoumi.' *Marine Policy,* 39, 191–200.

Furota, T. (2000) 'Distribution and feeding habit of tidal flat benthos.' *Gekkan Kaiyo*, 28(2), 166–177 (in Japanese).

Japan Fisheries Resource Conservation Association (2000) *Suisan yosui kijyun* [Standard for fisheries water]. Japan Fisheries Resource Conservation Association (in Japanese).

Kokubu, H., Okumira, H. and Matsuda, O. (2008) 'Historical changes in the tidal flat and its effects on benthos and sediment quality in Ago Bay.' *Journal of Japan Society on Water Environment*, 31(6), 305–311.

Kuwae, A. (2005) 'Development and self-stabilization of restored and created intertidal flat ecosystems.' *Journal of Environmental Systems and Engineering*, 35(790), 25–34.

Matsuda, O. (2010) 'Recent attempts towards environmental restoration of enclosed coastal seas: Ago Bay restoration project based on the new concept of satoumi.' *Bulletin of the Fisheries Research Agency*, 29, 9–18.

Matsuda, O. and Kokubu, H. (2011) *Towards satoumi in Ago Bay.* CBD Technical Series No. 61 (Biological and Cultural Diversity in Coastal Communities, Exploring the Potential of Satoumi for Implementing the Ecosystem Approach in the Japanese Archipelago), 62–69.

Ministry of Land, Infrastructure, Transport and Tourism (2002) *Syutoken hakusyo* [White paper on metropolitan area in FY2002], p. 22 (in Japanese).

Nature Conservation Bureau (1994) *Substructure investigation of natural environment*. Report of the coastal environment, pp. 2–8.

Secretariat of the Convention on Biological Diversity (2011) *Biological and cultural diversity in coastal communities: Exploring the potential of satoumi for implementing the ecosystem approach in the Japanese archipelago*. Montreal: CBD Technical Series No. 61.

Sohma, A., Sekiguchi, Y., Kuwae, T. and Nakamura, Y. (2008) 'A benthic-pelagic coupled ecosystem model to estimate the hypoxic estuary including tidal flats: Model description and validation of seasonal/daily dynamics.' *Ecological Modeling*, 215, 10–39.

Yanagi, T. (2007) *Sato-umi: A new concept of coastal sea management.* Tokyo: Terra Scientific Publishing Company.

9 Tidal flat restoration projects in Shima City and citizens' perceptions

Naoyuki Mikami and Hiromi Yamashita

9.1 Introduction

In Japan, tidal flats have long been exploited to create new land for farming, industry and housing; however, a significant proportion of the reclaimed land is now unused because of recent population decline. In response to this, Japan's first tidal flat restoration project involving unused reclaimed farmland was initiated in 2010 by local authorities and researchers in Ago Bay in Shima City, Mie Prefecture, as described in Chapters 7 and 8. Here, approximately 70% of the tidal flats have been lost to reclamation since the seventeenth century, and the pearl cultivation industry, which prospered particularly after World War II, led to marked environmental deterioration. An extensive survey identified 378 areas of unused reclaimed farmland that could be allocated as tidal flat restoration sites (Kokubu and Yamada, 2011). Pilot projects had already proved that restored tidal flats contribute to improved water quality and increased biodiversity (Kokubu and Takayama, 2012). Many of these sites could be turned into tidal flats simply by opening existing floodgates or removing sand dikes, without the need for large-scale construction work or significant expense (Figure 9.1). Furthermore, the tidal flat restoration programme is a major feature of the city's coastal management policy in Shima City's Satoumi Creation Basic Plan, established in 2011. Despite these favourable conditions, restoration projects have only been implemented in four out of the several hundred potential sites around the bay since 2010.

There have been very few attempts to investigate the sociological implications of tidal flat restoration in existing reclaimed land, particularly with regard to stakeholder perceptions of the risks and benefits of restoration projects and their potential impact on the community and local environment (Yamashita, 2015). Building upon the preceding two chapters, this chapter investigates factors underlying residents' attitudes

DOI: 10.4324/9780367863098-9

Figure 9.1 Removing sand dikes at the Wagu-ura tidal flat restoration site.

towards the tidal flat restoration projects in unused farmland in Ago Bay, using the results from qualitative and quantitative surveys in Shima City, and discusses the reason why it has been so difficult to implement the projects.

9.2 Research methods

The research was conducted using three methods. These were then applied to the other sites at Steart and Kuala Gula, in collaboration with our international colleagues who have contributed some of the preceding chapters of this book. First, we, the authors of this chapter, visited Shima City repeatedly from June 2011 and interviewed key local actors such as fishers, researchers, governmental and municipal officials and residents of the areas where the restoration projects were implemented. We also made participant observations at local meetings and events related to the tidal flat restoration programme, gathering relevant written material to support the interviews and participant observations.

Second, we conducted semi-structured interviews with the residents of Tategami, where the first restoration was implemented. They were conducted intensively in September and December 2015, five years after the project was launched, to investigate how the initiative had been perceived in the host community. The interview participants were recruited using snowball sampling, beginning with some of the key actors that one of the authors (Yamashita) interviewed in 2010. We were then able to complete the semi-structured interviews with 18 people in total, 5 women and 13 men, including those engaged in fisheries and other business areas.

Third, in February 2016 we conducted a questionnaire survey by post, targeting residents in all areas of Shima City; this mattered because the tidal flat restoration programme was promoted as part of the city's Satoumi Creation policy. With cooperation from the municipal government, 1,500 people were randomly selected from residents born on or before 1 April 2000 (N=47,437), that is, those in their first year of high school or older at the time of the survey. The questionnaire we sent out had 38 questions, covering issues like, (1) the respondent's overall relationship with the sea, such as their memories of the sea and impressions of tidal flats; (2) opinions on the tidal flat restoration projects; and (3) more general views about community development of Shima City. The response rate was 27.8% (n=417). The website links to the list of questions and the sampling methods are shared in Appendix 1.

9.3 Challenges perceived by neighbouring residents and others

From our interviews with residents near the first restoration site in Tategami, as well as others involved in the restoration programme, we found the unexpectedly slow progress of the restoration could be accounted for by several interrelated factors. The analysis and discussion of this chapter are adapted from and developed on Mikami and Yamashita (2017a, 2017b).

9.3.1 Coordination among stakeholders

Although little cost for construction work was attached to the restoration of unused reclaimed land, much effort was required to initiate and promote the restoration projects in local communities, including negotiations among the various stakeholders and administrative procedures necessary to change the land-use zoning. In the first restoration project in Tategami, the zone where seawater was introduced remained in public ownership, even after the reclamation. Although the second and third sites, both launched in 2012, were private properties owned by resort enterprises, they were willing to cooperate with the authorities in the restoration programme. In these initial cases, therefore, the landowners' agreement was not a significant issue. However, most of the remaining candidate sites for restoration are privately owned, and rights to the property can be conflicting and sometimes complicated due to deficiencies in property registration. It took about four years for negotiation among the parties concerned before the fourth project finally started in October 2016 in a candidate site in the Wagu area, which belongs to private landowners.

In addition, opening floodgates on reclaimed land requires permission from the prefectural governor, who is the coastal administrator, and the dikes and floodgates of reclaimed farmland are under the jurisdiction of the agricultural department of the prefecture. Although it initially seemed a matter of routine paperwork liaising with the prefecture, the Ministry of the Environment and Shima City, it soon became clear that support from a wide range of local residents was often necessary because they had been involved in the dikes being constructed, along with the direct landowners and leaseholders.

9.3.2 Costs and burdens that landowners and residents may have to bear

Landowners and local residents may have to bear a certain amount of responsibility in promoting restoration schemes. If the programme continues, much land is still categorised as agricultural on the official register, even if it has lain fallow for decades. In such cases, the owners who offer their land to the project would have to apply to convert it to another category, such as a pond, at their own expense. Even after complying with all these procedures, it is necessary to establish how a constant source of funding and necessary labour will be achieved to maintain and manage the newly created tidal flat over a long period. For example, repeated opening of a floodgate to allow seawater onto the site can make the area vulnerable to tsunamis and high tides, requiring the host community to perform careful floodgate management to prepare for potential risks. In addition, it will be necessary to monitor environmental changes regularly after the reintroduction of seawater and organise activities to utilise the restored tidal flats effectively, such as educational programmes and tourism. If the number of restored tidal flats drastically increases as expected, it is not realistic for the authorities to assume responsibility for the related maintenance, management and use of restored tidal flats alone; in other words, the host community may be required to take on some roles, possibly increasing residents' responsibility.

9.3.3 Unclear value to residents

Having taken these potential risks and necessary efforts into account, what value can tidal flat restoration projects provide in return, not in economic terms but to residents and communities as a whole? For example, bringing long abandoned farmland back into use for environmental restoration could provide a clear incentive to support the project. In an interview, the owner of a fallow rice field adjacent to the restored tidal flat in Tategami explained that he thought it would be better to cooperate with the restoration of the tidal flats than just let his farmland go to waste.

It is natural to assume, however, that it will become harder to maintain residents' positive attitudes if there are no tangible benefits. Some officials have suggested a reduction in real estate tax as an incentive for landowners to corporate with tidal flat restoration, but it has not been introduced yet. Since the beginning of the restoration programme, Shima City officials and local residents have dreamed of harvesting asari clams and seaweed on the restored tidal flats with local community organisations cultivating them and developing a recreational site for clam digging. As the questionnaire results in the next section suggest, an area where clam harvesting is possible is an image of the restored tidal flats that many local people had in common. However, even in the first restored site in Tategami, clam harvesting is not yet possible, and our interview survey with neighbouring residents in 2015, five years after opening the floodgate, indicated that they were losing interest in the restored tidal flats as well as in the restoration project.

The degree to which these costs and risks are regarded as tolerable depends on the residents' estimation of the value generated through the restoration projects. Local residents who do not highly value the results might think such costs and risks unacceptable and hesitate in becoming actively involved in the promotion of the projects. Based on these findings, we conducted a questionnaire survey of randomly selected residents from across Shima City to further explore factors underlying the differing attitudes towards tidal flat restoration projects.

9.4 Results from the resident questionnaire survey

The results from the questionnaire survey of the general population of Shima City show that approximately 50% of respondents were aware of the tidal flat restoration projects, with 74% in favour, with only 4% against and 23% undecided. The results also show the reasons why they supported the restoration projects were quite diverse. The respondents were asked to choose all applicable responses from 14 choices, and the most popular was "because it is helpful for cleaning the sea" (n=199), while reasons such as "it could become a place where we can play or learn" (n=138), "since it was originally part of the sea" (n=134) and "it is a good idea to utilise places we are not currently using" (n=125) were also common.

On the other hand, there seems to be greater consensus about success criteria for the tidal flat restoration projects. Among seven multiple choice options presented as indicators of success, only "restored tidal flat providing asari clams" was supported by a large majority (71.5%), while each of the other indicators was selected by fewer than half of the respondents. In Ago Bay, citizens used to enjoy gathering asari clams, so it represents a valued memory associated with the sea; it seems reasonable that these experiences form the basis of an image of restored tidal flats embraced by most of the residents. The support was particularly high among those in their forties and sixties, who may have actually enjoyed clam digging in the 1980s (see Table 9.1).

Although basic demographic factors (gender, age and occupation) do not appear to contribute to the differing attitudes towards the restoration projects, the primary factor was how much they knew about them. Out of all respondents who gave valid responses to both the awareness and attitude questions, 14.4% had heard about the projects and knew about them in detail, 35.8% did not know them well though they had heard of them and 49.8% had never heard of them. These three groups show quite different responses with regard to their attitudes towards the projects, as shown in Table 9.2. Those who were best informed about the projects were more supportive than the other two groups; among those who had never heard of the projects, around 35% were unsure whether to support them.

Table 9.1 Support rate of 'asari clams' as a success indicator across age groups

	Total number of respondents	*Those who consider 'restored tidal flat providing asari clams' as an indicator of success (the percentages show the rates in each age group)*	
Teens	9	5	55.6%
20s	24	13	54.2%
30s	35	22	62.9%
40s	41	33	80.5%
50s	73	55	75.3%
60s	107	84	78.5%
70s	81	55	67.9%
80s	38	28	73.7%
90s	2	0	0.0%
Total	410	295	72.0%

Table 9.2 Awareness of and attitudes towards the restoration projects in Ago Bay. Cross tabulation only of those who gave valid responses to both the awareness and attitude questions ($n = 402$)

		(Awareness) Did you know tidal flat restoration projects have been conducted in Ago Bay?			*Total*
		I have heard of them and know the details	*I have heard of them, but do not know the details*	*I have never heard of them*	
(Attitude) What do you think about tidal flat restoration projects in Ago Bay?	We should promote them	38 65.5%	59 41.0%	61 30.5%	158 39.3%
	If I had to choose, we should promote them	16 27.6%	63 43.8%	60 30.0%	139 34.6%
	If I had to choose, we should not promote them	3 5.2%	2 1.4%	5 2.5%	10 2.5%
	We should not promote them	0 0.0%	1 0.7%	3 1.5%	4 1.0%
	I do not know	1 1.7%	19 13.2%	71 35.5%	91 22.6%
Total		58 (14.4%)	144 (35.8%)	200 (49.8%)	402 100.0%

It seems likely that information is key to increasing support for the restoration projects, but it must also be noted that there were some respondents among those who knew about the projects in detail who showed weaker support or even disapproval, while 30–40% of those who did know much about the project expressed strong support. Therefore, people with the same level of information about the projects still differed in their attitudes towards the projects, indicating the existence of other underlying factors.

One such factor may be the residents' opinions on the development of Shima as a coastal city. To grasp their different opinions on various aspects of community development, we referred to the city's first Satoumi Creation Basic Plan, which designated three key areas in its satoumi policy: being able to earn (economy and industries), being able to learn (education and learning) and being able to play (recreation and public access). The authors chose nine major policy targets from these three areas (three targets from each area) and asked the respondents to indicate how important they felt each target was using a five-point scale (1=least important, 3=medium and 5=most important). Table 9.3 shows the results, listing the opinions of the supporters (restoration projects should be promoted); passive supporters (projects should be promoted if they had to choose); opponents (projects should not be promoted (including those who answered that they should not be promoted if they had to choose); and those undecided on whether they supported or opposed the restoration projects.

Focusing on the total average scores in the second column, we can see that all policy targets were generally regarded as important, with the highest score being 4.72 and the lowest 3.71. It should be noted, however, that targets regarding fisheries and other primary industries (items (a) and (c)) as well as recreation in and public access to the sea (items (g), (h) and (i)) were considered more important than ones regarding tourism industries (item (b)), or education and learning (items (d), (e) and (f)).

Having observed the general trends, we next considered how the respondents with differing attitudes towards the restoration projects regarded the importance of these nine policy targets. Using the analysis of variance (or the Kruskal–Wallis test when the data were not homoscedastic), we compared the average scores given to each target by the four groups of respondents. Eight policy targets out of the nine showed significant differences among the groups of respondents based on their differing attitudes towards the restoration projects.

Comparing the average scores given to each of the eight targets, we can see the differences among the scores were much higher for some targets than others. The targets regarding education and learning ((d), (e) and (f)) represented particularly wide gaps, no less than 0.5 difference between the supporters and passive supporters, as well as more than 1.5 difference between the supporters and opponents. On the other hand, the differences in the scores for other targets are rather small, particularly for those regarding recreation and public access.

9.5 Discussion

Based on the above, it follows that the importance one places on policy targets associated with the community development in Shima as a coastal city affects one's attitudes towards the tidal flat restoration projects. The

Table 9.3 Importance of major policy targets recognised by the respondents (average scores on five-point scale)

Groups of respondents / *Policy targets*	*All respondents (n=417)*	*Supporters of the projects (n=160)*	*Passive supporters of the projects (n=139)*	*(Passive) Opponents of the projects (n=14)*	*Do not know whether to support or not (n=94)*
(a) Establishing sustainable and stable fisheries*	4.44	4.63	4.33	4.21	4.35
(b) Boosting tourism using the sea*	4.03	4.24	3.96	3.21	3.91
(c) Training people to work in the primary industries*	4.33	4.60	4.13	4.14	4.24
(d) Strengthen study about satoumi in school education*	4.09	4.45	3.92	2.50	3.98
(e) Creating lifelong learning opportunities about satoumi*	3.88	4.22	3.72	2.43	3.75
(f) Providing learning opportunities for visitors*	3.71	4.13	3.50	2.57	3.49
(g) Upgrading shore environment for recreation*	4.33	4.53	4.25	3.36	4.24
(h) Creating rules regarding use of the sea*	4.31	4.46	4.15	4.50	4.27
(i) Promoting enlightenment activities for coastal clean-up	4.72	4.78	4.61	4.77	4.77

* Significant difference among the average scores for the four groups ($p<0.01$).

more important residents think these targets are, the more strongly they support the promotion of restoration projects. At the same time, targets regarding the development of the fishing and tourism industries, as well as securing public access to the sea are supported by a large majority of respondents, with fewer differences in opinion among the supporters, passive supporters and opponents. On the other hand, there was weaker support for the development of education and learning, both for children and adults, utilising satoumi resources (e.g. environmental education). Given these results, it can be assumed the differing attitudes to the community development of Shima as a coastal city, particularly those regarding education and learning, are one of the factors underlying the differing attitudes towards the tidal flat restoration projects. Those who emphasise the strategic importance of education and learning as part of community development will more strongly support the tidal flat restoration projects.

This observation naturally leads us to the question of why support for the tidal flat restoration projects appears to correlate more with the degree of emphasis on education and learning than with the other key areas of the satoumi policy. One explanation for this is found in the nature of the tidal flat restoration projects themselves. Although the steady implementation of tidal flat restoration will advance every target of the satoumi policy in the long run, it also seems reasonable to suppose that the short-term impacts of restoration projects may differ greatly among the various policy areas. In general, it takes a considerable amount of time to recognise the positive impacts that restored tidal flats have on fishing, pearl culture, the coastal environment and the tourism industry.

In addition, the increase in restored tidal flats will not directly promote recreation in and public access to the sea, as the potential sites for restoration projects are not necessarily suitable for recreational use by the general public. On the contrary, the promotion of education and learning on satoumi appears to represent a more immediate benefit of the restoration projects. In Ago Bay, there are already four sites where restoration work has begun, and the restored tidal flats have been utilised for various environmental education programmes for both children and adults. Thus, for those who emphasise the promotion of education and learning on satoumi, there are good reasons to support tidal flat restoration projects more strongly than others.

Our analysis has implications for the future promotion of tidal flat restoration in the city of Shima as well as nature restoration programmes in general. Overall, the present survey results indicate that attitudes towards tidal flat restoration projects are influenced not only by residents' awareness of the projects but also, more broadly speaking, by other factors including their attitudes towards community development. Expanding one's vision to encompass a broader perspective can help individuals evaluate the benefits of restoration projects in various dimensions: cultural or educational, as well as economic or industrial. Therefore, when attempting to advance restoration projects, it is essential that we provide sufficient opportunities for residents and other stakeholders to reflect on their vision of community development.

9.6 Conclusion: Implication for future practice and research needs

9.6.1 Implication for future practice

A few lessons can be drawn from the analysis of the Shima residents' opinions about the tidal flat restoration projects.

- The more people are aware of a project, the greater their support becomes. When you try to promote a restoration project, it is essential to effectively communicate the significance of it with local residents and to involve them in the process.
- There can be a variety of subtle obstacles to the progress of a project even when it does not pose conspicuous risks or significant costs. Overcoming such barriers requires a considerable amount of time and energy, particularly for negotiation and coordination among stakeholders.
- Clear presentation of the benefits of a project is essential to tackle such obstacles. Conversely, risks and costs will appear insurmountable when the public cannot appreciate the value of a project. The value does not have to be economic, but it is always important to show how the promotion of a project has significance in the development of a community.

9.6.2 Future research needs

Finally, future research should be expanded to explore more detailed understanding of public perception of the value of restoration projects. As mentioned above, clear presentation of the benefits is a crucial factor to promote restoration projects. However, what people consider and expect as benefits from a certain project develops from interaction among those involved in it, such as local residents, fishers, researchers and administrative officials. How it is possible for a local community like Shima to work out such a value could form the next piece of practice-oriented sociological research into costal wetland restoration.

References

Kokubu H. and Y. Takayama (2012) 'Evaluation of tidal flat restoration effect at coastal fallow fields in AGO Bay.' *Journal of Japan Society of Civil Engineers, Ser. B2 (Coastal Engineering)* 68(2), I_1091–I_1095 (in Japanese).

Kokubu, H. and H. Yamada (2011) 'Evaluation of tidal flat restoration effect in the coastal unused reclaimed area by promoting tidal exchange in Ago Bay.' *Journal of Japan Society of Civil Engineers, Ser. B2 (Coastal Engineering)*, 67(2): I_956–I_960 (in Japanese).

Mikami, N. and H. Yamashita (2017a) 'The slow progress of nature restoration projects: A case study of tidal flat restoration of unused coastal reclaimed land in Ago Bay.' *Journal of Environmental Sociology*, 23, 130–145 (in Japanese).

Mikami, N. and H. Yamashita (2017b) 'Factors underlying differing attitudes toward tidal flat restoration projects in unused farmland in Ago Bay: A survey of Shima City residents.' *Paper presented at the 6th International Symposium on Environmental Sociology in East Asia*. Taipei, Taiwan.

Yamashita, H. (2015) 'Social perceptions on the risks and benefits of tidal flat restorations: Weakness identified in the past research literature.' *Proceedings of the 5th International Symposium on Environmental Sociology in East Asia*, 289-298.

10 Opportunities for coastal wetland restoration and community development for the future

Hiromi Yamashita and Naoyuki Mikami

10.1 Perceived risks and benefits among citizens towards coastal restoration projects

This book focused on how local citizens in different parts of the world perceive and discuss the risks, benefits and sense of fairness in coastal wetland restoration projects on their shores, and how these perceptions change over time. We had the following three main questions in mind before starting the in-depth case studies in three different countries:

- How do people rationalise the risks and benefits of environmental restoration projects?
- How do people perceive a particular ecosystem to be restored?
- What are the implications of the findings for future practice and research?

All of the three sites discussed in this book relate to projects where land was returned to the sea, although they all used different terms, such as 'saltmarsh creation' (Steart, UK); 'mangrove rehabilitation' (Kuala Gula, Malaysia); and 'tidal flat restoration' (Shima city, Japan). Readers might, in the future, get involved in similar or other types of coastal wetland restoration projects and might welcome the opportunity to understand the reasoning behind the opinions citizens express for and against a restoration project.

Due to their differing history, culture and societal and economic situations, each site attracted different perceptions of the risks and benefits in their local restoration project. However, here we look at the main benefits that commonly appeared across all sites, which might be useful for future planning. Below, citizens who chose either 'strongly agree' or 'agree' to the relevant questions in the questionnaires are presented in brackets (for actual questionnaire content, see Yamashita & Mikami,

DOI: 10.4324/9780367863098-10

2016, 2018; Yamashita et al., 2018). Previous literature suggests that local people prefer individual and short-term benefits over wider and long-term benefits, but that was not the case in our findings.

Perceived benefits of coastal wetland restoration projects (% of respondents who chose this benefit): 101 total respondents in the Steart project, 81 in Kuala Gula and 417 in Shima:

- Increase in seafood production (21.7% in Steart; 58.0% in Kuala Gula; 28.0% in Shima)
- Creation of an area for recreation and education (85.1% in Steart; 48.1% in Kuala Gula; 33.0% in Shima)
- Natural disaster risk prevention (65.3% in Steart; 64.1% in Kuala Gula; the project in Shima was not designed for disaster prevention)
- Returning land to the sea (26.7% in Steart; 61.7% in Kuala Gula; 32.1% in Shima)
- Enhancing the local image (69.3% in Steart; 59.2% in Kuala Gula; 11.9% in Shima)
- Attracting visitors (58.4% in Steart; 59.2% in Kuala Gula; 6.4% in Shima)

Perceived risks of coastal wetland restoration projects:

- There are other priorities for tax revenue (4.9% in Steart; 2.6% in Shima; there was no such question at Kuala Gula, since funding comes from mixed sources)
- It is not helpful for improving the water quality of the sea (7% in Shima)
- It could cause food shortages in the long run (mentioned in the interviews in the Steart area)

Risk perceptions towards the restoration projects were mentioned by a small number of people. These feelings of risk and worry were not based on direct risks caused by the projects, but on worries about using up resources on them that should be used on something more important.

Flooding existing farmland was supported by around 30% of respondents in Steart and Shima: "It is ideal that we return it to the ocean if possible, since it was originally part of the sea" (26.7% strongly agree/agree; 36.6% neutral; 23.7% strongly disagree/disagree in Steart; 32.1% agreed with this statement in Shima). Also, in Steart the statement "the coastal environment is more important than keeping farmland", there was divided opinion (28.7% strongly agree/

agree; 46.5% neutral; 18.8% strongly disagree/disagree). Interestingly, in the statements about the relationship between the project and farmland in Steart, the respondents seemed ambivalent. However, usually the respondents showed a pattern of agreeing with positive statements about the Steart Marshes project and disagreeing with negative statements in general.

From the statement saying the project "represents a loss of productive farmland", it seems that the citizens did not take sides in choosing which environment is more important, fishing grounds or farming (34.6% strongly agree/agree; 24.7% neutral; 28.7% strongly disagree/disagree in Steart). One criticism of the project in Steart came from a perceived risk of future food shortages, with an increasing world population and food insecurity in the context of globalisation. The citizens seemed to be aware, yet were reluctant to get involved in this dichotomy, although sympathy towards losing farmland was present.

10.2 What elements of judgement do local people use for coastal wetland restoration projects?

In the in-depth interviews, when citizens discussed the perceived risks and benefits of the project and their reasoning, they often used similar judgement elements across the three sites. Those elements are about underlying philosophies or views towards nature. Also, interestingly, positive and negative feelings towards the project sometimes had a common root in the same past event. The difference was only how the person perceived and experienced it.

Opinions for and against are formed by multilayered judgements on various elements, and below we have summarised them. These factors fell into five main discourse areas: (1) view of nature; (2) worries about loss; (3) lifestyle choices; (4) a fair decision-making process; and (5) a fair distribution of risks and benefits. These judgement factors include both person and group/community perceptions. One site might not have all these factors from which citizens could make judgements on the project. However, it might be useful for a project officer to understand these points, when exploring local opinions in depth.

After looking into these factors, we could quickly understand that citizens could not be simply separated into groups for and against, and this approach could be framed as confrontational. Instead, considering how flexible a project is in taking into account as many of these aspects as possible, would make a project much more sensitive to citizens' worries and expectations (Table 10.1).

Table 10.1 Citizens' judgement factors on restoration projects

Judgement factors	*Details (both personal and community)*
1. View of nature	① Valuing a particular ecosystem (understanding its importance) ② Whether nature is something to be restored or not (nature evolves around human need vs human need within the ecosystem) ③ Acceptance of existing environment (e.g. '*I don't like the current environment, but I'm used to it*') ④ Acceptance at not seeing the outcome for a long time (e.g. '*I think it's a good idea, but it would take hundreds of years to complete, wouldn't it?*')
2. Worries about loss	⑤ What has been or could be lost (personally/in the community/wider world) (e.g. original ecosystem, existing ecosystem, houses being flooded, food productivity, tranquillity) ⑥ Compensation mechanism for unexpected outcomes
3. Lifestyle choices	⑦ Impact on income (positive/negative) ⑧ Opportunities for new challenges (e.g. meeting new people, speaking English to tourists to the site) ⑨ Educational opportunities for children and adults ⑩ Enrichment of leisure and family time ⑪ Bringing back happy memories (e.g. tastes and activities which people enjoyed in the past or as children)
4. A fair decision-making process	⑫ Transparent consultation process (openness, minutes, approach, changes made according to citizens' requests) ⑬ Trust towards the project contractors (e.g. sincerity, communications skills of the project contractors) ⑭ Consistency in policies for external events
5. A fair distribution of risks and benefits	⑮ Fair usage of tax or public funding ⑯ Predicted benefits distributed fairly (e.g. not seen as only spending money on a certain part of the community) ⑰ Predicted risks distributed fairly ⑱ Regaining fairness (e.g. undoing past 'wrongs', balancing others' loss, why do only they receive benefits?) ⑲ Feeling good about doing good for others (passing on something good for future generations) ⑳ Opportunities to create social cohesion (e.g. through communication and discussion on community developments)

Kawase (2018) states that in qualitative welfare trade-off discussions, one needs to look at the ethicality of the trade-off by looking at the characteristics and relationships of the welfare being exchanged. He offers three viewpoints: time closeness, characteristic sameness and direct relationships, since risk–benefit comparisons are very much linked with autonomy, welfare and justice. Interestingly, our research results also showed autonomy, welfare and justice as the main elements citizens employ in making judgements. Habermas tells us that we should "not expect a generally valid answer when we ask what is good for me, or good for us, or good for them; we must rather ask: what is equally good for all?" (Habermas, 1996, p. 248). The data also showed how this project could be good for all; the issues of fair distribution seem to be one of the core questions citizens are asking, whether consciously or not.

10.3 What general images do citizens have towards coastal wetlands?

Regardless of their distances from the restoration sites, citizens generally had positive images of their coastal wetlands. Across the sites, citizens chose 'beautiful' (around 45% in Steart; 76.5% in Kuala Gula), 'want to go' (around 80% in Kuala Gula) and 'many living creatures' (69.3% in Steart; 82.7% in Kuala Gula; 59.9% in Shima). The number of people who said mangroves are smelly (37% in Kuala Gula) was overtaken by those who said they are not (60.5%). The perceptions towards coastal wetlands remained positive, even when nearly 80% of respondents in Kuala Gula chose there are 'many mosquitoes' in mangroves.

At the same time, there were people who thought their coastal wetlands were 'dirty' (15.0% in Shima); 'there are no living creatures' (9.2% in Shima); and 'I don't want to go' (10.6% in Shima). Some chose the term 'sludge' to describe their wetlands (around 25% in Steart; 36.0% in Shima). How close citizens were to wetlands in their day-to-day lives seems to have increased their fondness of them. The percentage of people who chose 'I want to go' to mangroves was highest in the Malay community (80.0%), who fish and host mangrove restoration activities. All respondents of this Malay community chose people 'can collect food' in the mangroves, and many chose 'can raise animals or fish'. On a similar note, one respondent in Shima wrote that the tidal flat was "an area that supports Shima City's finances". Even with the same scenery, individual citizens have different views and attachments to their wetlands. In Steart, saltmarsh is a 'man-made/altered habitat' and 'untidy, spoilt countryside' for some, but for others a 'diverse changing environment' and a 'beautiful changing landscape'.

10.4 Which coastal wetland ecosystem services are people aware of?

People's perceptions towards the risks and benefits depended on their contexts, including the relationship they had with the ecosystem in the past, how they saw the ecosystem services of the restored place and the project's aims. The citizens were more aware of the various ecosystem services of coastal wetlands than we or past researchers imagined. The wetland functions chosen by a majority of the respondents were: 'provides areas for birds to rest or feed' (90.1% in Steart; 68.2% in Shima); 'reduces damage from storms and flooding' (70.3% in Steart; 80.2% in Kuala Gula); 'provides space for animal to graze' (62.4% in Steart); and 'prevents coastal erosion' (60.4% in Steart). Understanding that coastal wetlands could have carbon capture mechanisms was the least regarded ecosystem service across all the projects: 'reduces CO_2 released into the atmosphere' (19.8% in Steart).

Understanding about the regulating services that oceans provide was a clear difference between the fishing and non-fishing communities.

Table 10.2 Characteristics of citizens who tend to support coastal wetland restoration projects

Characteristics of people	*Any evidence of supporting restoration projects?*
People who live closer to the project?	No. People living far away from the project equally support the restoration projects. There is no significant difference between people's support and how far away they live.
People who are aware of the restoration project?	Yes. The people who know about the restoration project tend to support the project more.
People who have positive images of coastal wetlands?	Yes. Those who have positive images of coastal wetlands tend to support the project more.
People who understand the ecosystem services of coastal wetlands?	Yes. The more a person knows about their wetlands' ecosystem services, the more support they express.
People who are younger or older?	No. There is no significant difference among different age groups in supporting restoration projects.
People who see the coastal environment getting worse?	No. It seems that other factors are stronger than if they see the coastal environment is getting worse or better.
People who trust the project contractors	Yes. Those who do not have trust in the project contractors do not support the project

Coastal wetlands are seen to 'support fisheries' (79.0% in Kuala Gula); 'enrich ocean biodiversity' (76.5% in Kuala Gula; 54.9% in Shima); and 'provides a nursery habitat for growing fish' (75.3% in Kuala Gula) in the sites that have active fishing industries. To understand this ecosystem service, one needs to know about the regulating ecosystem service of coastal wetlands and the food chain, such as 'it supports phytoplankton and seaweed which feed other living creatures'. However, in Steart, where unfortunately traditional fishing activities have disappeared over the last 30–40 years, only 43.0% of the respondents reported that saltmarshes can 'provide a nursery habitat for growing fish' and 'enrich ocean biodiversity'. Only 17.8% of the respondents agreed that saltmarshes can help to 'clean seawater' and 'provide food' (4.0%).

Many of us would be also curious about who usually supports coastal wetland restoration projects. Although this is hardly generalisable, we summarised what we can say from the data (Table 10.2).

10.5 What success indicators would citizens like to judge restoration projects?

Through this work we hoped to start building up the participatory success indicators for wetland restoration projects. The data were collected in the interviews and questionnaires, which asked the respondents to choose or describe how they would consider whether a restoration project was a success. Table 10.3 summarises the main success indicators as mentioned in each case study site.

There is a tendency for successful indicators to be like the project aims. However, several citizens' indicators show interesting criteria. For example, in Steart, "being an attractive space for recreation and exercise" was not the main project aim and was a supplementary target. However, it was one of the main success indicators for citizens in judging the project's effectiveness in the future, after the criteria of "enhancing biodiversity". "Reducing the risk of flooding" was one of the motivations in the area closest to the sea wall; however, in the wider community, risk reduction was not seen as a strong success indicator.

In Kuala Gula, many respondents did not come up with a success indicator in the questionnaire, but those that did respond were concerned about the size and the state of the mangroves, using the terms 'more', 'beautiful' and 'healthy'. Interestingly, the phrases they used seem to suggest that the more mangrove forests there are, the better the community becomes.

In Shima, local people thought the return of asari clams, which they used to enjoy collecting, would be a very strong project success indicator, as well as harvesting aosa seaweed. Asari clams need not only

Table 10.3 Participatory success indicator development by citizens

	Steart	*Kuala Gula*	*Shima*
Results	• Enhancing biodiversity and wildlife, including birds (41.5%) • An attractive space for recreation and exercise (30.6%) • Reducing the risk of flooding (14.8%) • Providing a space for learning and education (11.8%) • Being a local attraction (6.9%) • Project not successful (5.9%) • Reducing dangerous driving and noise (2.9%) • New cycle path from another village (2.9%) • Maintaining current good management (2.9%)	• Area of mangrove increased and managed well (19.7%) • This area became more beautiful and lovely (9.8%) • Sea production increased and a clean sea (8.6%) • More tourists coming (6.1%) • More birds in the area (4.9%) • Seeing many fish in the mangroves (3.7%) • Wild animals and beautiful birds able to remain (2.4%) • Kuala Gula has been developed (2.4%) • Preventing coastal erosion (2.4%)	• Restored tidal flat providing asari clams (71.4%) • Restored tidal flat becoming an environmental education site (47.7%) • Restored tidal flat providing an area for aosa seaweed (46.5%) • Place to play or rest (38.6%) • Reduction of red tide (35.7%) • Enhance image of Shima City (26.6% • It goes back to how it was originally (9%)
Indicator species	Biodiversity in general, and birds	Mangrove forest itself, crabs, fish and shrimp	Asari clams and aosa seaweed
Project aim	Mitigating effects of the nearby port development on mudflats, creating site for migratory birds, building new sea walls for local community	Rehabilitation of oceanic biodiversity, prevention of tsunami disasters, creation of education site and community managed forest site, turning planting activities into a tourist attraction	Rehabilitation of tidal flats' water purification mechanisms, enhancing oceanic biodiversity, creation of environmental education site

Table 10.3 Cont.

	Steart	*Kuala Gula*	*Shima*
Question asked	Q11. Please describe how you would consider the Steart Marshes project to be a success? (open question)	Q12. What would you like to see if the Mangrove Rehabilitation Project is successful? (open question)	Q20. What kinds of effects in the future might make you think that a restoration project was successful (6 multiple choice questions plus free writing)

Table 10.4 Citizens' seven success indicators of coastal wetland restorations

Citizens' seven success indicators for coastal wetland restorations

- Size and quality of the restoration site increasing
- Number of indicator species increasing
- An environment clean enough to produce healthy food (if possible, in quantity)
- Going back to or creating a time when people can enjoy direct contact with wetlands (e.g. touching, eating, swimming, looking)
- Community being protected from the targeted risks
- Having an attractive space for recreation and education
- Enhanced local image, which leads to further community development

tidal flats, but also conditions such as a flow of nutrients, a healthy wider ocean and a specific water temperature range. Harvesting asari clams has been very difficult all over Japan in the last decade. So, to have this as a success indicator means the citizens have high expectations and also have had direct experience of happy times on tidal flats and a close relationship with them in the past. Also, it shows that citizens view tidal flats as somewhere where food can be harvested, with an environment that is clean enough to produce food to eat. We have summarised the citizens' success indicators for coastal wetland restorations although this will keep evolving as any future research is completed (Table 10.4).

10.6 Implications for future coastal wetland restoration projects

This book looked at various aspects of citizens' perceptions towards nature restoration projects. Hopefully, each chapter provided something interesting for a future project of yours. Here, we provide seven summaries of implications for future practice, before discussing the importance of future research activities.

Point 1: Being aware of positivity towards nature restoration projects in the community

The first thing we would like to say is please enjoy the positivity towards nature restoration projects to be found in communities. We came across extremely positive perceptions among citizens, with most residents understanding both the coastal wetland ecosystem services and the rationale behind the restoration projects for the long-term benefits of the wider community. Interestingly, these positive perceptions were often not felt by the project contractors or those in the policy-making arena. Restoration project workers need not be too defensive on arriving in a community, nor feel the need to 'educate' locals, although of course advising citizens about things they might not know will form part of their remit. Positive attitudes could avoid unnecessary cycles of misunderstanding and begin the process of getting to know one another.

Point 2: Citizens hoping to see long-term and wider benefits from the project

Past studies have often indicated that citizens are in a way 'selfish', and often only motivated by personal gain during a restoration project. However, our study results suggest otherwise. Many citizens care about the biodiversity and ecological recovery of their environment so they might then appear slightly frustrated if they cannot see positive trends emerging a few years after a project's completion. A project needs to provide a range of indicators as evidence to ensure expectations are realistic, gaining long-term support.

Point 3: Creating opportunities to turn locals' concerns into opportunities

A common characteristic of these three sites was the project contractors' openness to criticism and worries in the local communities. They had the capacity to turn those concerns into positive changes, including how the site was designed and used. Locals could voice their opinions and solutions could be reached together with the contractors. For example, the Steart project changed the route of the sea wall to preserve a pond, which was the site of a memorial for a local family's deceased son. Local representatives were also invited to the government office to draw a possible footpath route after voicing their concerns, and the car parks were placed strategically to deter visitors from driving into the village. There were administrative and financial costs attached to this, but ultimately these concerns resulted in improvements to the site. To achieve these positive changes, the amount of autonomy and budgetary margins given to the site manager and the contractors is crucial.

Point 4: Being aware of which 'community' we are talking about

When we talk about the 'community', we often mean the area closest to the project, or the villages we can see from the main road. But in Kuala Gula, when we randomly chose where to start the questionnaire activities, we came across areas we had not seen in previous visits and found citizens who had never encountered local activities due to societal and language barriers. We met foreign workers, citizens living in the plantation community, elderly citizens in houses behind high gates and others living on the water where the foundations were shaking due to soil erosion. The Malaysia project coordinator, who is the lead author of Chapter 5, said the first thing he did after moving to the village was to visit all the houses to say hello individually. To us, as researchers, seeing all the different faces greeting us to share their ideas was simply refreshing. Only then, did we feel we could talk about the 'community'.

Point 5: Opening up informal communication opportunities and eating together

Another common learning opportunity across the sites was keeping consultation channels between citizens and project contractors, including non-governmental organisations (NGOs) and governmental officers, always open. In Kuala Gula, the project worker lived on site for three years with his family. The local people saw him and his family in their villages, and if there were any concerns, they could always talk to him as a friend. For the citizens, their acceptance of the project was not only about the ecosystem services it could provide, but also whether the project workers were 'nice' and 'approachable'. In addition, how often citizens had opportunities to meet with the project contractors had positive impacts on their perceptions. In the UK, the contractors opened their office for a drop-in session every Friday and sometimes had a BBQ with the residents. These frequent opportunities for citizens to be able to talk about their concerns and ideas at informal events worked well for smoother understanding across different stakeholders.

Point 6: Local perception change: Creating a mechanism to maintain contact after a project's completion

Local citizens' perceptions towards restoration are constantly changing. They are influenced by various events, such as weather (e.g. nearby flooding); political discussions (e.g. local politicians or the media supporting the project); and hearsay. Once negative perceptions towards a project happen, it could bring back past memories of conflicts in the community. Unlike in conventional construction projects, completion of the hard engineering on site marks the start of the main restoration activities. The site changes over time, and for some will look much worse for a while. This can be especially difficult for those who do not know how the ecosystem looked before the land was reclaimed, and it is hard to imagine the outcome. Meanwhile, some might expect the changes and restoration to happen more quickly and become frustrated with the slow pace of change.

These frustrations and speculations sometimes accumulate as questions or even as anger towards a project. Here, it is important to keep clear channels of communication open between the project contractor and the citizens, even after the completion date. At Steart Marshes, the project manager was replaced by a site manager after completion of the construction part of the project, together with a communications officer who works on education and maintaining relationships with locals and volunteers. Having such personnel or clear local representatives in the community opens up the possibility that a project could keep capturing future changes in the community perceptions towards it.

Point 7: Protecting a project's reputation by tackling external issues

Social perceptions towards a project are also influenced by what is happening beyond the project. The Kuala Gula project went through a difficult stage when nearby mangrove forests were cut down to create a shrimp farm for foreign export. Locals experienced pollution from the site and this reduced the significance of the benefits from their mangrove restoration project. At the same time, some locals voiced their frustration that the restoration project could not stop the destruction nearby. Taking action or standing up to something happening beyond the project could be challenging. The locals come from different backgrounds, and the trust built among them in the project could be jeopardised if they feel they are not working together against those causing the damage.

10.7 Future research activities cherishing subjectivity and objectivity

How the public will respond to a restoration project continues to be a major concern among those who want to promote nature restoration projects in the future. The amount of research work in this area is still limited and there are many aspects left for social scientists to explore. We are currently investigating saltmarsh restoration projects that have been delayed or suspended due to issues between project workers and citizens in the UK. To encourage many more research projects in social perception studies in the future, we would like to finish by making three suggestions.

First, designing the research activities to cherish and capture the 'subjectivity' of respondents' answers is encouraged. Often local people give opinions that might initially appear as very subjective, but they are often based on legitimate reasoning and past experiences. Spend time in understanding what they are trying to convey. In terms of interview structures, questionnaire content and places to gather data, ensure the research design is prepared to capture citizens' unexpected thoughts to further develop understanding of the communities.

At the same time, the 'objectivity' of the data sampling is important. Due to time and funding constraints, it would be difficult for many research projects to hear the voices of everyone in a community. Therefore, random sampling, which aims to generate a representative sample, is also necessary to make sure that the data gathered are useful for future researchers and policy makers (for more information on how we struggled to achieve this in different ways, see Appendix 1 and 2).

Third, creating funding, space and opportunities to engage practitioners on the inside as researchers would enhance the work in this field of social scientific studies on nature restorations enormously. At all the sites in this book, the practitioners, consciously or not, utilised their skills to capture social perceptions and responded to them, but lack of time to write up and analyse their experiences is a common problem, reducing the opportunity to enhance understanding in this field.

Coastal wetland restoration projects have the potential to provide multiple ecosystem services and disaster prevention benefits, as well as to encourage community development with a positive focus on their wetlands. It is interesting for us, policymakers, project workers and other researchers to unpack these positive and negative local perceptions, and the process will give us interesting clues on how humans could live together with nature.

References

Kawase, T. (2018) Risk benefit evaluation of clinical research. *Chiba University Law Articles*, 33(2), 163–202.

Habermas, J. (1996) *Between facts and norms: Contributions to a discourse theory of law and democracy*, trans. William Rehg. Cambridge, Massachusetts: MIT Press.

Yamashita, H., and Mikami, N. (2016) *Survey of the sea of Shima and community development "You, the Sea and Tidal flats" questionnaire first analysis summary report*. Ritsumeikan Research Repository (in English and Japanese).

Yamashita, H., and Mikami, N. (2018) *Survey of public perceptions of the coastal area and mangrove rehabilitation project in Kuala Gula, Malaysia*, first analysis summary report. Ritsumeikan Research Repository (in English, Malay, Chinese, and Japanese).

Yamashita, H., Mikami, N., McInnes, R., Everard, M., and Pham, T. H. (2018) *Survey of public perceptions of the coastal marshes and mudflat restoration project, UK "You, the Estuary and Steart Marshes" questionnaire first analysis summary report*. Ritsumeikan Research Repository (in English and Japanese).

Appendix 1: Summary of the objective questionnaire sampling strategies in rural communities

This research project used three different sampling methods used to access rural populations as objectively as possible: simple random sampling, multi-stage sampling with exhaustive distributions to all houses and multi-stage sampling with area sampling. Each method was set after consideration of the local situation, such as the availability of population data, communities separated due to ethnicities or occupations, literacy levels, language variation, local postal mechanisms and research budgets. The following writing introduces the challenges faced in terms of the sampling and data collection methods at the three separate sites, and how we addressed them.

Sampling strategy A: Simple random sampling at Shima City, Japan

The target area for this survey was set as the whole of Shima City. Data collection challenges at this site included:

- Due to budget constraints, the research project could not afford to send the questionnaire to everyone in the city. The targeted population was large; therefore, the sampling method needed to be as objective as possible to ensure the reliability of the data collected.
- The population register in the municipal office includes individual citizens' dates of birth and addresses; however, the researchers were not allowed access to the data directly.
- The project also wanted to access pupils at high schools (15–18 years old) to understand young people's opinions, since some of them leave the city just after finishing their upper secondary school.

The above challenges were overcome with the cooperation of the Shima City Municipal Office. To avoid the researchers directly dealing with the citizens' personal information, the officers at the municipal office conducted a random sampling of 1,500 residents born before 1 April 2000 from the basic resident register (at the time of the research, all the respondents were older than 1st grade upper secondary students).

- Population to be selected: 52,913 people (population on 1 February 2016)
- Targeted population: 47,437 people (those born before 1 April 2000)
- Numbers of selected population: 1,500 people

The return rate of this work was 27.8%, with 417 valid responses. The data came back from all the districts with a similar return rate and age group variations.

Sampling strategy B: Exhaustive with multiple sampling in Somerset, England

The data collection was conducted between 1 July and 15 August 2018. Data collection challenges at this site included:

- Access to the resident register was not possible.
- Due to the lack of public transport and the relatively large area to cover, it could be difficult and costly for the research team to distribute the questionnaires to each house by hand.
- It was decided that neither the environmental non-governmental organisation (NGO) nor the Environment Agency, who were taking the lead, should be directly involved in the data collection to make the citizens more comfortable in expressing their opinions towards the project; this was a well-known project which in the past created some tensions in the communities. Also, the NGO and the Environment Agency hoped to obtain as objective citizens' perspectives as possible.
- It was unclear if the residents would trust researchers from overseas.

The above issues were overcome by support received from a local university professor, who joined the research team and let the project utilise his contacts for returned questionnaires. Also, the research team built a relationship with the local parish councillors and those who deliver the local newsletter once or twice a month. They allowed the research team to write a small piece in their newsletter with a photo of the researcher. The survey was posted together with the latest community newsletter, which carried the short article written by the researchers. Sedgemoor District Council also agreed to us saying that this work was supported by them to develop trust among the recipients.

The accompanying form asked that one person from each household be picked as a representative of the household to complete the survey, and that they should be aged 15 or older, ideally the person with their birthday closest to 1 January. If there was only one resident in the household, that person became the representative. The return rate of this work was 24.2%, with 101 valid responses. The highest return rate by district (50%) was from the community directly next to the restoration project. Although it was an unsolicited contact, the comment sections were often very interesting and lengthy.

Sampling strategy C: Area and multi-stage sampling in Kuala Gula, Malaysia

This was the most challenging site in this whole research project. Data collection issues to overcome at this site included:

- Access to all the people; the issue of literacy was anticipated.
- The postal service is not reliable in the area; therefore, the postal questionnaire system would not work.
- Multiple languages are spoken in the area (e.g. Malay, Chinese and English).
- To cover the different languages and obtain friendly access, the research team needed to hire and train local people on conducting structured interview (questionnaire) activities and research ethics.
- Each community is separated in terms of schooling, places to eat, places to pray and places to shop and get together, and the plantation workers usually stay within the plantation company compound. The research team needed to negotiate a way into the plantation communities.
- Originally the research team planned and brought aerial photographs of the research area to identify the numbers of houses and chose which houses to visit by running random numbers (stratified random sampling). However, this did not work since on site we found many of the roofs did not represent residential houses, but sheds for storing boats and seafood production factories. Also, there were many buildings housing sparrows, bred for their nests as a delicacy in Chinese food.

The timescale for this questionnaire was from 14 to 19 September 2017. The questionnaire survey was targeted at people over 15 years old who lived in the Kuala Gula District. Randomly selected respondents were visited at their home, and their answers were collected either by the structured interview method or by the distribution survey method. Since it was not possible to conduct random sampling of the respondents through tools such as a basic resident register (information about all the residents in the area), the research team chose the second-best way to randomly sample respondents.

First of all, we obtained the estimated population of the six communities within Kuala Gula through interviews with the local government office and the head of the village. At the same time, the research team decided upon the target number of 80 respondents for this survey activity. We then allocated this number of 'required responses' to each community according to the size of population.

Second, the precise point of the research area within each community was randomly selected. The RAND function of Excel produced randomised numbers by using longitude and latitude (decimal system) within each selected community geographical area. These precise points were used as a sampling starting point in each community. These were plotted on a Google map then the houses closest to these points in a circular catchment were selected to be approached to obtain one questionnaire response from each. Up to ten answers from ten households around one starting point were collected. When the research team needed to sample more than ten households from one community, the second or third starting points were chosen randomly again.

To reduce bias, it was important that the respondent from the household was also chosen at random and that the researcher did not just speak to the person who answered the door. At each house, the research team member asked the first person they talked to pick out an unseen number. In this case, they were written on spoons with one spoon for each family member older than 15 years old. The person in the house who should answer the questionnaire was decided by which number they happened to choose (for example, where there were three household members older than 15 years old, if a representative picked the number one, the oldest person in the house was chosen to answer the questionnaire) (Figure D.1).

This method was very effective in terms of reaching those who are not in the house during the daytime or daughters or young people who tend not to have opportunities to reply to questionnaires because they are not considered representative of the household. Through the above method, 81 responses were obtained across all of the six communities within Kuala Gula District as planned (Table D.1).

We hope that the record of our attempts in the field will help you with your future research in conducting objective questionnaire sampling, despite various difficulties in rural communities. For more details of the sites information, questionnaire contents and results, please refer to our questionnaire reports (see Yamashita and Mikami, 2016; 2018; Yamashita et al., 2018).

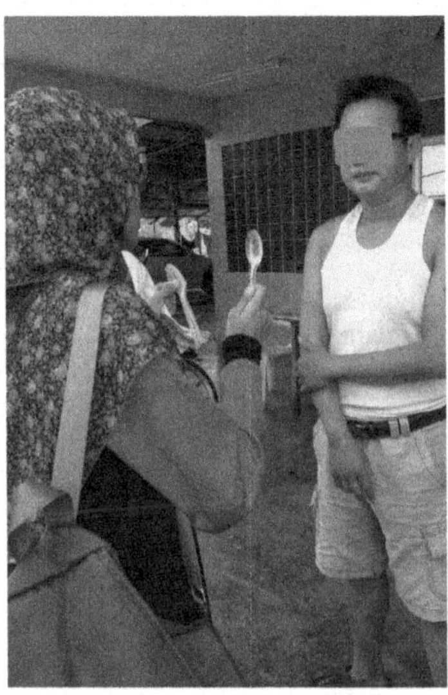

Figure D.1 Researchers in the field asking a person at the door.

Table D.1 Summary of the sampling and the case study sites

	Shima City, Japan	*Steart Peninsula, England*	*Kuala Gula, Malaysia*
Sampling	Simple random	Cluster sampling	Area (stratified random) and multi-stage
Population	52,913	996	6,370
Accuracy of population data	Down to his/her birthday and almost all the residents	Household numbers were known to the local newsletter deliverers	Rough guess work from the head of the villages
Access to the official population data	Yes	No	No
Literacy	High	High	Low to high (variable)

(*continued*)

Table D.1 Cont.

	Shima City, Japan	*Steart Peninsula, England*	*Kuala Gula, Malaysia*
Languages	Japanese	English	Malay, Chinese, Tamil, and English
Postal mechanisms	Yes	Yes	No
Methods of access	Postal survey to randomly selected individuals (unsolicited contact but with the City's approval and logo)	Postal survey (unsolicited contact but with the local newsletter)	Face-to-face survey (structured interview)
Assurances of the randomness within the household	n/a	Birthday method	Numbered spoon and draw method
Prizes	Prize draw	Prize draw	Small present to every respondent
Number of questions in the questionnaire (including personal details)	38	19	22

References

Yamashita, H., and Mikami, N. (2016) *Survey of the sea of Shima and community development "You, the Sea and Tidal flats" questionnaire first analysis summary report*. Ritsumeikan Research Repository. (in English and Japanese).

Yamashita, H., and Mikami, N. (2018) *Survey of public perceptions of the coastal area and mangrove rehabilitation project in Kuala Gula, Malaysia, first analysis summary report*. Ritsumeikan Research Repository. (in English, Malay, Chinese and Japanese).

Yamashita, H., Mikami, N., McInnes, R., Everard, M., and Pham, T. H. (2018) *Survey of public perceptions of the coastal marshes and mudflat restoration project, UK "You, the Estuary and Steart Marshes" questionnaire first analysis summary report*. Ritsumeikan Research Repository (in English and Japanese).

Appendix 2: An example of the questionnaire contents (Steart Marshes)

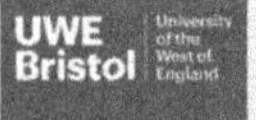

Questionnaire about You, the Estuary and Steart Marshes

Supported by the Sedgemoor District Council, we are independent researchers from universities in Bristol and Japan who have conducted similar studies in Malaysia and Japan.

We are looking for someone aged 15 or older, ideally whose birthday is the closest to 1st January, to complete this survey as a representative of the views of the household. (If you live alone, you are the representative!)

Your answers will form a part of the important international research work.

If you are interested, at the end of the survey you can enter the prize draw with a chance to win a £20 voucher. The information you give us will remain anonymous. Thank you.

If you prefer the online form to fill in, please visit here or scan the QR code: https://goo.gl/forms/sCTsr28ONOcfkbcH3

Deadline for posting the survey: 31 July 2018

Let's begin!

Q1. What do you think of the coastal environment in and around the Severn Estuary? *(Please circle one answer)*

1. Getting better 2. Not changing 3. Getting worse 4. I do not know

Q2. Salt marshes are coastal wetlands dominated by short, salt-tolerant plants and mud that are regularly flooded by tides. What mental image do you have of salt marshes?
(Please circle ALL choices that apply)

Sludge, Beaches, Want to go, Do not want to go, Many living creatures, No living creatures, Beautiful, Dirty, Can collect food, Cannot collect food, Smelly, Not smelly, Can graze animals, Cannot graze animals,

Others [Please specify:...]

Q3. What functions do you think salt marshes have?
(Please circle ALL that apply)

1. Cleans seawater
2. Supports fisheries
3. Provides a nursery habitat for growing fish
4. Provides wood
5. Enriches ocean biodiversity
6. Reduces damage from storms and flooding
7. Prevents coastal erosion
8. Reduces CO2 released into the atmosphere
9. Provides an area where people can have fun
10. Provides areas for birds to rest or feed
11. Provides space for animals to graze
12. Others [Please specify: ....]

Q4. Mudflats are areas where mud or sand which are regularly flooded by the tide and do not have any vegetation. What mental image do you have of mudflats?
(Please circle ALL that apply)

Sludge, Beaches, Want to go, Do not want to go, Many living creatures, No living creatures, Beautiful, Dirty, Can collect food, Cannot collect food, Smelly, Not smelly, Can graze animals, Cannot graze animals,

Others [Please specify:...]

Q5. What functions do you think mudflats have? *(Please circle ALL that apply)*

1. Cleans seawater
2. Supports fisheries
3. Provides a nursery habitat for growing fish
4. Provides wood
5. Enriches ocean biodiversity
6. Reduces damage from storms and flooding
7. Prevents coastal erosion
8. Reduces CO2 released into the atmosphere
9. Provides an area where people can have fun
10. Provides areas for birds to rest or feed
11. Provides space for animals to graze
12. Others [Please specify: ....]

Q6. On Steart Peninsula, a salt marsh and mudflat rehabilitation (coastal realignment) project has been conducted by re-flooding farmland. Do you know about this project?

1. I have heard about it and know a lot about it
2. I have heard about it, but do not know much about it
3. I have never heard about it

Q7. Have you, your family, your relatives or your friends visited the Steart Marshes site since September 2014? *(Please circle ALL that apply)*

1. I have 2. My family or relatives have 3. My friends have 4. No one I know has

Q8. Did you or your family own or farm the land sold to conduct this Steart Marshes project? *(Please circle ALL the choices that apply)*

1. Myself or my family used to own land
2. Myself or my family used to farm on the land
3. None of the above

Q9. What do you feel about the Steart Marshes project?

1. I feel very positive about the project 2. I feel positive about the project
3. I feel negative about the project 4. I feel very negative about the project
5. I do not know

Q10. Consider the following statements about the Steart Marshes project and indicate to what extent you agree or disagree to each one. *(please tick appropriate)*

The Steart Marshes project …	Strongly agree	Agree	Neutral	Disagree	Strongly disagree	Don't know
1. promotes seafood production						
2. reduces the effects of natural disasters						
3. creates a place where we can play or learn						
4. vitalizes the local economy by attracting many visitors from outside the area						
5. deprives the local residents of a quiet living environment by introducing too many visitors						
6. has been implemented through a fair consultation process						
7. compensates for the damage caused by other coastal developments						
8. boosts the image of Steart Peninsula or Sedgemoor District						
9. helps us to prepare for climate change						
10. represents a loss of productive farmland						
11. is desirable since it returns farmland to the sea, which was the original state						
12. enhances the coastal environment which is more important than keeping farmland						
13. is a waste of public money						

Q11. Please describe how you would consider the Steart Marshes project to be a success:

....

....

Q12. Do you want to participate in Steart Marshes restoration activities in the future?

1. Yes 2. No

Q13. Please tell us about any other opinions or suggestions you have on the Steart Marshes project or related issues.

[Please describe: ....]

Finally, we would briefly like to ask about you.

Q14. Please *circle* **your age group.**

1. 15–19 years old 6. 60s 11. Prefer not to say
2. 20s 7. 70s
3. 30s 8. 80s
4. 40s 9. 90s
5. 50s 10. 100s

Q15. What is your sex?

1. Male 2. Female 3. Other................ 4. Prefer not to say

Q16. Please choose the area you live in at the moment.

1. Steart 2. Stockland Bristol 3. Otterhampton 4. Combwich 5. Pawlett

Q17. Roughly how many years have you lived in Sedgemoor District?

[Please specify: ....years]

Q18. What is your job status at the moment?

1. Employed by someone 2. Self-employed 3. Retired/pensioned 4. Student
5. Unemployed 6. Other [Please specify: ....]

Q19. [Those who answered 1 or 2 in Q19] Which category below fits best with your type of occupation? *(Please circle ONE)*

Agriculture and related work; Fishery and related work; Mining and manufacturing; Electricity provision; Water supply; Construction; Wholesale; Transport; Education; Accommodation and food service; Communication; Finance and insurance; Real estate; Scientific and technical activities; Public administration; Health and social work; Other [please specify: ....]

Index

Note: Page numbers in *italics* indicate figures and in **bold** indicate tables on the corresponding pages.

Ago Bay Tidal Flat Restoration Projects: activities of 97–98; area background 89–92, **90–91**; beauty of Shima City and 93–94, *94*; building win-win relationships with other governmental departments and the public 115–118, *116*, **117**; challenges and opportunities seized during population and environmental decline 94–96, *95–96*; conclusions on 100–101; conditions of unused reclaimed areas before restoration through **106**, 106–107, *107*; implications for future practice and research needs 101–102, 118–119; introduction to 103–104, *104–105*, **105**; learning from promoting 98–100; main trial opening the floodgate 110–114, *111–113*; other successful tidal flat restoration projects like 114–115; project summary 87, *88–89*; simple random sampling 147–148, **151–152**; small-scale trial using water pumps *108–109*, 108–110; status of utilisation of tidal flats and reclaimed areas in Ago Bay and 92; success indicators for 139–141, **140–141**; trials in 107–114, *108–109*, *111–113*; *see also* tidal flat restoration projects, citizen perceptions of

Arnstein, S. R. 3

Belmont report 8

climate change 4

coastal squeeze 27

coastal wetlands: current extent of 17–18; current rates of degradation and loss of 18; drivers of degradation and loss of 18–20; general images citizens have towards 137; people's awareness of **138**, 138–139; restoration fit in addressing current status and trends of 20; status and trends in 17–20

coastal wetlands restoration: benefits and challenges in 20–23; versus conservation 11–12, **11–12**; contributions to global agendas 22; current indicators of success for 7–8; elements of judgment used by local people for 135–137, **136**; future research activities cherishing subjectivity and objectivity 145; general risk-benefit principle and its limitations in 8–9; implications for future 141–144; methods discussed 4, *5*; not being more widely implemented 22–23; past research on social perceptions of 7, 9–11; perceived risks and benefits among citizens towards 81, 133–135; social perceptions of 1–3, *3*; success indicators for judging

139–141, **140–141**; terms used for 5–7; *see also* social perceptions
Communication, education, participation and awareness (CEPA) programme 72–73, *73*
community development 14, 61, 123, 127–128, 130–131, **136**, **141**, 145
conservation projects 11–12, **11–12**
controlled reduced tide (CRT) 6
Curado, G. 9, 10

Davidson, N. C. 17
deficit model of citizens 10

education 8, 10, 53, 64, 66, 70–72, *71–72*, 75–77, 124, 128–131; CEPA programme 72–73, *73*; encouraging resident participation in 98, *104*; *see also* environmental education
England *see* Steart Coastal Managed Realignment Project
environmental education 22, 58, **63**, **90**, 115, 119, 130, **140**
Esteves, L. S. 10
Everard, M. 13, 23

Finlayson, C. M. 17
Framework Convention on Climate Change, United Nations 22

Goeldner-Gianella, L. 10–11
Gofman, J. W. 8

Hart, R. A. 2
Hurricane Katrina 21

Indian Ocean Tsunami 21
Ishibuchi restoration project **90**, 106, **106**, 108, 110, *111*, 114–115

Japan *see* Ago Bay Tidal Flat Restoration Projects

Kawase, T. 137
Kuala Gula Mangrove Rehabilitation Project: activities for livelihood development 71–72, *72*; area and multi-stage sampling 149–152, *151*, **151–152**; background 61–64, *62–63*, **63**, **65**, 79; Communication, education, participation and awareness (CEPA) programme 72–73, *73*; community and environmental sustainability 73–74; discussion of benefits of 85–86; findings on 81–85, **82–83**, **85**; focus of 69–70, *71*; implications for future practice and research needs 74–77, 86; local and tourism resources 66; in Malaysian context 67–69; perceived risks and benefits of 133–134; as protected site 74; research methods on public perception of 80–81; success indicators for 139–141, **140–141**
Kokubu, H. 14, 92, 98, 103, 106, 121

ladder of participation 2–3, *3*, 74, 101
local community skill base 39–40

managed retreat 6
mangroved 13, 17, 19, 21–22, 133, 137–144. *see also* Kuala Gula Mangrove Rehabilitation Project
Malaysia *see* Kuala Gula Mangrove Rehabilitation Project
McGrath, T. 13
McInnes, R. J. 55
Mikami, N. 13–14, 123, 133–134, 152
Mississippi Deltaic Plan 21
Myatt, L. B. 10–11

National Appropriate Mitigation Actions (NAMAs) 22
National Determined Contributions (NDCs) 22
Niu-no-Ike restoration project **90**, 114

Otani-ura restoration project **90**, 114–115

Paris Agreement 22
participation: citizen 2, 81; community 72–73, 76; by consultation 2; defining 3; encouraging resident 98; functional 2; interactive 2; ladder of 2–3, *3*, 74, 101; for material incentives 2; oppotrunities of 10; passive 2;

public 2; self-mobilisation/active 2; top-down 2
participation styles 2–3, *3*
perceptions *see* social perceptions
Perumal, B. 13
Pimbert, M. P. 2
Pretty, J. N. 2
public perceptions *see* social perceptions

Ramsar Convention Secretariat 4, 17, 22
re-flooding 6
regulated tidal exchange (RTE) 6
Renn, O. 2
restoration *see* coastal wetlands restoration
risk-benefit principle 8–9
risk and benefit 1–4, 7, 10; evaluation indicators 47; expression of individual 48–49, **48**, *49*, 57; fair distribution of **136**; general risk-benefit principle 8–9; global agendas and 22–23; perception of 81–82, **82**, 133–135

sampling 14, 57, 80, **106**, 108, 110, 123, 145, 147–152, **151–152**
saltmarshes 13, 17–19, 22, 27, 30, 36, 41, 43, 54, 145; defined 137; mental image of 51–52, *51–52*, 57; public perception of 139
Sendai Framework for Disaster Risk Reduction 22
Sigma Plan 21
Simenstad, C. 23
social perceptions 1–3, *3*; Ago Bay Tidal Flat Restoration Projects 95–96, 98–100; and awareness of coastal wetland ecosystem services **138**, 138–139; challenges and risks perceived by neighbouring residents 81–82, **82**, 123–125; changes of 82–84, **83**; general images towards coast wetlands 137; implications for future practice and research needs 57–58, 141–144; Kuala Gula Mangrove Rehabilitation Project 79–86, **82–83**, **85**; levels of enthusiasm for project across different villages 84–85, **85**; mental images and function 50–53, *51–52*; past research on 7, 9–11; perceived risks and benefits among citizens 81, 133–135; project success indicators (*see* success indicators); Steart Coastal Management Project 46–47, 50–58, *51–52*, **54**, *56*; success indicators in 139–141, **140–141**; tidal flat restoration projects 121–132, *122*, **126–127**, **129**; understanding ecosystem services 53–55, **54**
Society of Ecological Restoration (SER) 7–8
Steart Coastal Managed Realignment Project: area background 27–28, **28**, 33–34; determining consultation styles for 37–38; early stage engagement 34–36; as exemplar of engagement and design 41–42; findings from individual and group interviews on 46–50; findings from questionnaire data 50–55, *51–52*, **54**; implication for future practice and research need 42–43; perceived risks and benefits of 134–135; project success indicators defined by citizens 55–56, *56*; project summary 29–31, *29–31*, 46–47; providing additional societal benefits 40–41; questionnaire contents 153–155; research methods 46–47; research on public perception of 46–47; sampling strategy 148–149, **151–152**; success indicators for 139–141, **140–141**; working with skill base from local community 39–40
success indicators 14, 53, 55–56, **126**, 139–141, **140–141**
Sustainable Development Goals (SDGs), United Nations 20, 22

Terada, R. 8
terminology of coastal wetland restoration 5–7

Thomas, K. 10
tidal flat *109*: status of utilisation of 92
tidal flat restoration projects, citizen perceptions of: challenges perceived by neighbouring residents and others 123–125; discussion of 128–131, **129**; implication for future practice and research needs 131–132; introduction to 121–122, *122*; research methods 122–123; results from resident questionnaire survey 125–128, **126–127**; *see also* Shima Ago Bay Tidal Flat Restoration Projects

Uranaka, H. 13, 96–97

volunteers 39–40, 42, 86, 98, 101, 115, 117, 144

Wagu-ura restoration project **90**, 115, *122*
Wildfowl & Wetlands Trust (WWT) 34–36; determining consultation styles 37–38; working with skill base from local community 39–40
win-win relationships, governmental/public 115–118, *116*, **117**

Yanagi, T. 96
Yamashita, H. 9, 13–14, 121, 123, 133–134

Printed in the United States
by Baker & Taylor Publisher Services